ATROPOS PRESS
new york • dresden

© 2015 by Am Johal
Think Media EGS Series is supported by the European Graduate School

Cover Design: Peggy Bloomer
Cover Photo: Sierra Bloomer

ATROPOS PRESS
New York • Dresden

151 First Avenue # 14, New York, N.Y. 10003

all rights reserved

978-1-940813-92-9

Ecological Metapolitics:

Badiou and the Anthropocene

By

Am Johal

ACKNOWLEDGEMENTS

I would like to thank a wonderful community of colleagues at the European Graduate School and Simon Fraser University in Vancouver, Canada who provided generous guidance to me throughout the writing process. I would like to thank Alain Badiou for providing inspiration to take on this topic as a result of his seminars in August of 2012 at the European Graduate School. I had already chosen this area as a topic, but the discussions from his seminars provided an important opening to explore these questions from a novel angle.

The completion of this book would not have been possible without the wonderful community of people in Vancouver and elsewhere of academics, artists and activists who provided guidance, inspiration and the occasional drink when necessary. Thank you to Samir Gandesha, Jeff Derksen, Jamie Hilder, Dan Adleman, Giorgio Agamben, Judith Butler, Hilda Fernandez, Jeremy Fernando, Wolfgang Schirmacher, Glen Coulthard, Matt Hern, Benjamin Bratton, Avital Ronell, Catherine Malabou, Nicholas Perrin and Althea Thauberger for either generous readings of my work, or providing invaluable insights along the way in seminars.

Special thanks to Andrea Actis and Patricia Reed for their generous assistance in thoughtfully editing my work in various stages.

Table of Contents

PREFACE

*T*his book interfaces Alain Badiou's philosophical work on militant political change with the contemporary question of ecology and the geological epoch referred to as the Anthropocene. Building on Badiou's broader philosophical ontology, *Ecological Metapolitics* will be introduced as a philosophical term, defined as the consequences a philosophy is capable of drawing from the political project of ecology as thought. Concepts of democratic materialism, human rights, democracy and ethics will be critiqued, exposing the limits of existing political philosophy. The discussion applies a methodology of *affirmative dialectics* to today's ecological questions, considering them from the perspective of the event, political change and the subject. Through such framing, Badiou's philosophical contributions are situated within current ecological discourses. Discussions on resistance, the *passion for the real,* sovereignty, accelerationism and geo-engineering are also considered in the book. Though Badiou's oeuvre evidently figures prominently in my treatment, it is also complemented by thinkers such as Michel Foucault, Giorgio Agamben, Judith Butler, Glen Coulthard, Frantz Fanon, Carl Schmitt and others.

INTRODUCTION

*W*hile the history of ecological thought and the relation between humanity and Nature within continental philosophy extends back to the Greeks, the geological epoch known as the Anthropocene presents new challenges to thinking through the question of being and non-being today. Our new condition scrambles old ways of thinking through the problem, and brings new possibilities to the forefront. The Anthropocene urgently foregrounds the necessity for new ideas concerning age-old philosophical questions: *what is it to live;* the human relation to *death*; the human relation to Nature; and the human relation to other species. The Anthropocene brings back old philosophical questions in a new frame. The question of ecology today is properly a question of ontology, the science of *being qua being*, in the philosophical field.

Broadly speaking, Alain Badiou's philosophical work considers processes of militant political change, the formation of the subject and the event, through what he identifies as the truth procedures of politics, love, science and art. Through a re-reading of Hegelian dialectics, Marxism and Structuralism, his work addresses the *subject* and the *real*. The influences of Plato, Sartre, Althusser and Lacan, resonate throughout his work but his thinking also takes a considerable distance from each of them as well, developing a philosophical ontology that is uniquely his own.

While Badiou is not viewed as an ecological thinker or someone thinking through 'Anthropocenic' problems (having commented or lectured only sparingly on the issue), he is nonetheless an innovative thinker to map onto these pressing ecological questions. The aim of this book is precisely to interface Badiou's philosophical work with the contemporary question of ecology, placing his work in dialogue with other thinkers as

9

to what philosophy can offer to the discourse, beyond the same-old *Environmental Ethics* readers. Though I will not focus on Badiou's set theoretical proofs, it is my position that Badiou's ontology and, more broadly, his work on thinking militant political change, has much to contribute to the current crisis.

Of course, thinking through ecology in philosophy is not an attempt to *suture* philosophy to politics – in the parlance of Badiou, such a move would constitute a disaster of thinking. In mapping Badiou's work upon the discourses and problem of ecology today, a conceptual space opens up to think through the problem philosophically at a topological level – what I call *Ecological Metapolitics*. In responding to questions, Badiou has often remarked that the contemporary problem of ecology is properly a political one. He has, however, also lectured on the matter, teasing out what he views as the properly philosophical problems at stake in ecology. Given the mutual interpenetration of these fields, the book proceeds through five chapters.

The book departs by looking closely at Badiou's limited work directly related to ecology and places it within his lifelong project of *thinking militant political change* so as to grasp the stakes of what he brings anew to the question. As the question of ecology today is also an existential one, the book will discuss the idea of death, the death of God, and mourning. Ultimately terms such as ecology and my own term, *Ecological Metapolitics*, will be newly defined in the process.

Secondly, the book will follow Badiou's ongoing critique of what he refers to as *democratic materialism.* This idea, in my view, is crucial to deconstructing the ecological impasse and what is done in the name of democracy, political philosophy, human rights, and ethics. Badiou's ontology provides a useful clearing procedure to open up philosophical space to think the problem of ecology today in a radically deconsecrated realm.

Thirdly, this book looks at the philosophical history of thinking the idea of *resistance,* through a number of theorists in the philosophical field in order to reimagine the question of ecology within the current historical context, locating Badiou's ontology in relation to others. Badiou views the problem of ecology as properly being a question inside the emergence of the subject of the event.

The fourth section addresses geopolitics, sovereignty and the *limit point* of change, where, Badiou reminds us, inside the desire for change is also the fear of the *passion for the real*. Ecology also opens up spatial and temporal scalar problems that will be discussed. Geopolitics and spatial ordering, combined with new confrontations related to the very idea of national sovereignty, emerge at a global scale while impacting localization. The work of Carl Schmitt, Benjamin Bratton and the movement known as Accelerationism is brought in to the fray of ecology, geopolitics and sovereignty, alongside Badiou's work.

Finally, the problem of ecology is then woven through the ideas of *Karl Marx*, the *Frankfurt School*, and a critical analysis of the possibility of contemporary collective interventions through emergent technological possibilities, such as *geo-engineering*. In conclusion, we return to Badiou, giving him the last word on what philosophy may have to offer the problem of ecology today, summarizing as it were the parameters framing the project of *Ecological Metapolitics*.

1

BADIOU, ECOLOGY, AND THE SUBJECT OF CHANGE

Change

Although Alain Badiou has not directly written or lectured widely on the topic of ecology, his *thinking* of emancipatory politics through his body of philosophical work can nonetheless be sufficiently aligned with current questions in ecological discourse today. Expanding from his few lectures and writings on ecology as a conceptual starting point, definitions of both *ecology* and, what I am calling *Ecological Metapolitics,* will be established. These definitions are built around the idea that humanity is a part of Nature and not apart from it, but also, that humans are unique beings on the earth who, unlike other species, have a singular capacity to destroy all living beings on earth. Although the human animal has a dependent relationship to Nature, Nature does not require the human animal; Nature itself has the capacity to destroy the world and living beings as well. In this formulation of ecology, necessary philosophical questions emerge concerning the relation between Nature and history, as well as the very possibility of the continuation of the collective world of living beings as such.

The contemporary Western world is the inheritor of the Enlightenment idea that history is a struggle against Nature and that change involves dominion over Nature. Following Badiou, located within the problem of ecology today is a call for the invention of *a new modern tradition*, where ecology is positioned as a question properly inside the subject, rather than a question inside of Nature. In ecology, there is a desire to transmit the conditions of existence toward the future, towards the continuation of existence as such, yet it is also a desire to move beyond "the monstrous human desire for newness."[1] For Badiou, within ecology, is a will for a new tradition that constitutes a revolution of the revolutionary tradition itself: ultimately, it is an attempt to invent *a new modern tradition*. Described this way, ecology is both "a rupture with the modern world and a rupture with the revolutionary tradition"[2]; it is the "means of the modern world mobilized inside the contradiction of history and nature."[3] *Nature, as it will be defined here, concerns the earth and all its phenomena in the material world, existing independently, with or without, human activity or civilization.*

Badiou speaks of the dialectic, between *change* and *immobility*, and between *change* and *tradition*.[4] He argues that, "tradition is something that does not organize change but rather organizes a sort of struggle against the change."[5] Change can be a disruption on the side of accelerating the capitalist world *as it is*, so it can also work against the continued existence of the collective. For Badiou, change regarding the question of ecology must be tied to the concept of *equality* in order to have relevance in philosophy. In an interview with Oliver Feltham, Badiou frames his concerns with ecology in this way:

> Let's start by stating that after 'rights of man,' the rise of 'the rights of Nature' is a contemporary form of the opium of the people. It is an only slightly camouflaged religion: the millenarian terror, concern for everything save the properly political destiny of peoples, new instruments for the control of everyday life, the fear of death of catastrophes…It is a gigantic operation in the depoliticization of subjects….Nature is therefore in no way a norm situated above humanity. We will inevitably make decisions according to the diversity of our interests. Ecology solely concerns me inasmuch as it can be proven that it is an intrinsic dimension of the politics of the emancipation of humanity. For the moment I do not see such proof.[6]

Beginning with a consideration of ecology, Badiou asks, "What is a change? What is a true change? What is a false change? Is change better than immobility?...What is a change in society?...What is a change in life?, And what is a change in private life?" [7] The idea of change in ecology, in its contemporary form, is a human construction according to Badiou. Nature, as it were, does not think change of its own accord. Ecology is a human construction that attempts to think through the problem of the relationship between humanity and Nature through a subject, and to reiterate, this is precisely why ecology is properly a question inside the subject. Bruno Bosteels observes, that for Badiou, "truth is first of all a process or a labour, rather than an act of revelation or a propositional attribute...the practice of philosophy...amount[s] to thinking the truths of one's time, truths that have occurred before the arrival of the philosopher on the scene of the event."[8] Politics, love, science, and art produce truths without philosophy in Badiou's ontology; they are what he calls *conditions*. Badiou proposes that the philosophical task "is to organize inside the subject the struggle against false change or bad change."[9] It is to build resilience against the terror of the *common ideology,* which can be defined as the ideology of *the world as it is—democratic materialism* under the finitude of capitalism. This struggle against change, on the side of tradition, he names the "conservative change"—"a change toward continuity, conservation."[10] Badiou presents this not as a passive operation, but as an active one to "affirm the necessity of the repetition."[11] Michel Serres, in *The Natural Contract,* writes, "At stake is the Earth in its totality and humanity, collectively. Global history enters nature; global nature enters history: this is something utterly new in philosophy." [12] Within ecology is the consideration of the tragic magnitude of anticipation, decision and memory of the collective human subject in the world. It is also a relationship to the future and those not yet living.

Badiou shifts the question of humanity, change and Nature into its contemporary form: *ecology*. The destruction of Nature by humankind is, by all definition, on the side of change, where current forms of capital circulation, resource extraction, and human domination over Nature are repetitions of a specific type of change. For Badiou, the ecological vision of a repetition of the natural world and the continuation of the species beyond the sphere of the singular human animal is on the side of tradition. This, it would appear, is a counterintuitive category of truths: conservationist ecology, although revolutionary, attempts to preserve tradition (repetition of Nature). Logically speaking, to persist in the destruction of Nature is identical to the change inside of capitalistic logic. Reinforcing Nature's repetition would be a new tradition within the conservative idea of change for Badiou. The move to establish the repetition of Nature as such, in overcoming the violence and destruction organized by humanity over Nature, involves the invention of *a new modern tradition*.[13]

A New Modern Tradition

Badiou contrasts what he terms as a *tradition,* against that of the classical revolutionary vision that he argues is on the side of change. Badiou places ecology in the context of a *traditional revolution* by articulating it as "a revolution of the tradition itself."[14] In ecology, there is a desire for a *new, modern tradition.* The classical revolutionary idea is also a tradition—a tradition of change, supporting the idea that the old world must be destroyed. Inside the desire for a new tradition in ecology is "the possibility of a future which is not only composed of change but also of continuity and repetition,"[15] in other words it does not aim to "create a new form of pure progress or of pure becoming."[16]

As a question probing the relation between *Nature* and *history,*[17] ecology must cope with its inheritance of the Enlightenment ideal (at least within a Western context) that history is a struggle against Nature where change involves a dominion over Nature. In the processes that structure such a relation, there is not only the destruction of Nature, but of civilizations, languages, cultures, other species and geographies that are on the side of tradition. The task of ecology today is not a return to a world of pure repetition and pure tradition; rather, it is the arduous task of ecology to create a *new modern tradition.* Badiou takes the position that this *new modern tradition* is not a movement from the past to the present, but from the present to the future—"an attempt to create a future which is not the continuation of pure change, of destructive change."[18]

Badiou's formulation of ecology posits a new relation between history and Nature to include all living beings and the natural world, and not (importantly) exclusively of the anthropocentric vision of the world. The separation of history and Nature is refuted in this vision of ecology; instead, this new vision calls for their mutual entanglement. That humankind is the master of Nature as part of the Enlightenment tradition (affirmed by the likes of René Descartes and Francis Bacon) forms the logic of the terror of common ideology today. Ecology must propose a break from this tradition, but this does not entail a world of *pure* repetition and *pure* tradition. Instead, inside the desire for a new tradition in ecology must be "the possibility of a future which is not only composed of change but also of continuity and repetition."[19]

Gilles Lipovetsky, in *Power of Repetition*, writes of repetition in this way:

> a paradox: it is in a second chance occurrence that necessity arrives, when the constellations of pulsional or discursive bodies find themselves blocked, stabilized, when *repetition* replaces unpredictable movements of attraction and repulsion. Then comes the concept, the symptom, the affective dispositifs – and simultaneous with these effects, the institution of negation, since every stable formation, *qua permanent,* continually *excludes* the *same* combinations. Such is the very operation of power: not so much exclusion, inevitably implicated in every complex of bodies qua determinate assemblage, as the repetition of exclusion, a repetition inscribing a *fixed order.* So that power is found ready made in its entirety in the sphere of affects or thoughts once the latter are constituted in iterative configurations, thus producing an *order* which does away with the formation of new combinations, the chaotic movement of bodies, the play of chemical chance. That all power entertains a specific relation to time and to chance, this is what seems to us essential in *Libidinal Economy...* To the point, as we shall see, where the essential function of the general systems of powers, even within the framework of capitalism, will be to retain time—that is, to administer or to impose mere production.[20]

Badiou argues that the problem of a treaty between Nature and history is that humankind is on both sides. Nature does not speak; it is mute according to Badiou, so the question of ecology and its attendant relation between history and Nature is a way of humankind negotiating with itself.[21] It could be argued that the tsunamis, earthquakes, weather occurrences, and loss of species can be considered a form of communication by Nature of a *catastrophe to come*, or it could be humans signifying Nature retroactively. This would, however, place too much emphasis on one side or the other of the Nature/history coin without working through their imbroglios. In this light, the contemporary problem of ecology, I would argue, is a human construction whose possible solution is dependent upon a becoming subject. And, as we know from Badiou, such a subject is only born in fidelity to an event.

What Is It To Live?

With Badiou, we return to one of Plato's founding questions for philosophy: *What is it to live?* Ecology raises this question once again in a novel way, demanding of us to define our relation to the future and to Nature in our own time. Our task for a philosophy adequate to the problem of ecology is to continue with the Platonic thread, which, in Badiou's account of it, "was based on the idea the only life worth living is one oriented by an idea and by our participation in a truth procedure."[22] With the question of ecology, we are once again in Plato's cave since change is also concerned with questions of power, knowledge, and truth. As Badiou argues,

> the fundamental propaganda of power is the claim that we must stay inside because it is rational, reasonable and necessary to stay inside… my claim is that we must begin with the idea that power, the state, and the institutions of power, are on the inside of the cave…Power has a relation to change because it articulates what change is really possible.[23]

Badiou also warns of the consequences of what is called a *crisis*, and asks us to pay particular attention to how crises are defined, and in whose interest. He writes, "there is propaganda concerning the idea of crisis today. Today, a crisis is something which is good for the inside"[24], suggesting that we must first determine what is *inside* and what is *outside* the repetition of the common ideology, in order to adequately speculate on change at all.

The question of ecology is about a change to the modern world itself. In Badiou's formulation, "a dialectical tradition is not repetition, it is the preservation of the new relationship between tradition and change."[25] Human civilization, and the repetition it constructs in the modern world today, is at war with Nature. The work to change the world regarding the problem of ecology is a "desire for a new tradition, inside of which there is the possibility of a future which is not only composed of change but also of continuity and repetition."[26] Badiou argues that "we must transmit the conditions of this existence for the future, for the continuation of existence as such…it is the struggle to continue the pure existence of the collective."[27] This idea of change, both political and theoretical, also involves a subject that has a particular task to distinguish between good and bad forms of change. As Badiou elaborates,

> It is to organize inside the subject the struggle against false change, or bad change. And it is to organize in the subject the return to the good repetition, or the good life inside the repetition."[28]

There is a relation to the future being proposed, one which implies a change in the human relation to the present. If being, or Heidegger's notion of *Dasein*, is part of a present *being-there*, how can we propose this movement of *being-there* to the *future-being-now*, without doing violence to the *being-there*? How does one adequately transmit today the conditions of the *future world*? Is one to negate living in the present world and conduct one's life for the future of Nature? Is one to construct a new world and a new subject that is living for the *future world*? How can we do this without constructing a *passion for the real* that is the neo-authoritarian legacy of the last century?

Within the question of ecology there is a danger of moving from the terror of the common ideology (what Badiou identifies as *democratic materialism*) to the *passion for the real* from the last century. The danger lays in the (possible) production of a new terror, a reactionary terror; both on the side of Nature and on the side of *democratic materialism*. This relation to an uncertain future, the possibility of collective finitude or civilizational extinction, and the baggage of the last century's *passion for the real,* creates a dialectical tension between *courage* and *anxiety.* The narratives surrounding ecology are also part of a long messianic tradition of the *end-of-days prophecies;* as well, ecology can also fall victim to a messianic *waiting for-the-event,* an almost religious or spiritual conviction expectant of an *immanent future.* The quest for the realization of ecological consciousness can also create a kind of simulacrum of the event—gestures of which we see in such greenwashing phenomena as "sustainable" capitalism, "ethical" mining, and "green" oil refineries[29] —whose slogans and terms transmit a rudimentary affect without any real disruption or systemic change to the world. Thus ecology can easily be transformed sophistically into a luxury commodity, or become a marketing technique of corporate branding. There is a slipperiness of terminologies in circulation today regarding the question of ecology that philosophy is tasked with antagonizing and interrogating.

Philosophy as Affirmative Dialectic

Badiou views philosophy as having a crucial role as an affirmative construction of truth created from the event and the fidelity of the subject to the consequences of the event. In *The Communist Hypothesis*, he writes:

> When the world is violently enchanted by the absolute consequences of a paradox of being, the whole of the domain of appearing, threatened with the local destruction of a customary evaluation, must come again to constitute a different distribution of what exists and what does not… under the eruption being exerts on its own appearing, nothing in a world can come to pass except the possibility— mingling existence and destruction—of another world.[30]

For Badiou, it is the task of the philosopher to be optimistic. Change is always possible as the world is constructed by a series of situations involving beings and sequences of singularity as a consequence of the event. The belief of the *abolition of future* as such, is viewed as a false, nihilistic construction for Badiou. Change is not impossible—it is *always* possible. In *Manifesto for Philosophy*, he admits, "it is not known how to make thought out of the fact that man has become irreversibly 'master and possessor' of nature."[31] But with a rupture in democratic materialism, Badiou argues that, "today's task...is to support the creation of such a discipline subtracted from the grip of the state, the creation of a thoroughly political discipline."[32]

Badiou proposes, as a first sequence, that philosophy as a means of thinking change should begin as an affirmative dialectic. To challenge Hegelian dialectics, he presents a model of philosophy that begins with an affirmation but still employs negation after the initial affirmative sequence. Through its particular dialectical sequence, negation of the situational definition by the state and capital is achieved through affirmative construction and subtraction. Through and against Spinoza's idea of philosophy as pure creation, Badiou's case for an affirmative dialectic is a two-fold attempt to move beyond the limitation of Hegel's dialectic whilst working around Nietzsche's dialectic between *ressentiment* and *affirmation*. However, it may be argued that Hegelian negativity makes an uncanny return precisely through the desire for the real framed by Lacan. For Badiou, there is a problem in reinvesting logic inside of itself; there must be an affirmation of the positive before negation as the initial dialectical movement. Something of the future *precedes* the present.[33] Badiou argues that we must struggle, but that we must also reassess the value of negation for our own context: "we cannot create without negation but we can create with less negation than before, and with less negation than the last century."[34]

The classical dialectical relationship fundamentally relies on negation. The Hegelian dialectical framework, in its relation between affirmation and negation, ultimately relies on a movement of *creation through negation*. Badiou observes, through Lenin, that revolutionary consciousness is "basically the consciousness that one stands in a relation of negation to the existing order."[35] Yet, he asserts, the negative dialectics found in Adorno, for example, is a model revering the "suffering human body," that ends up generating a "moralism…perfectly adequate to capitalist domination under the mask of democracy."[36] However, it should be mentioned against dramatic simplification, that even Adorno's negative dialectics are not pure negation – they are intended to be part of an affirmative construction after the initial negation. What Badiouian dialectics ultimately propose, is to swap the order of classical dialectical logic, where affirmation precedes negation, where the "future comes before the negative present."[37]

Negation, as it were, should come as a result of "the consequences of the birth of the new subjectivity, and not the other way around; it is not the new subjectivity that is a consequence of the negation."[38] The creativity of negation, then, is not the first move. Rather, the event is the creation of the new possibility of the situation, the first move of which is to "create a new body and affirm a new subjectivity."[39]

It is imperative to create something new inside the new situation that calls upon affirmation and division, rather than the traditional movement from negation to affirmation. The event is that which interrupts the law and creates the possibility for a new world. Inside the situation of the event is the opening of a new possibility, where the event is the materialization of the consequences of this new possibility. There is a new subjective body created by the eventual rupture. Fidelity to the event and the material consequences and construction of its possibility are the crucial task of the subject to the event.

The Problem of Ecology and the Task for Philosophy

For the question of ecology, global warming emerges as a new kind of localizable event that materializes over time and space at the scale of the infinite; it is a new kind of event for the modern world as such. Since the common understanding of an event is that it is temporally bound, the durational nature of climate change raises new questions by its premise. Wolfgang Schirmacher approaches the question of ecology by positing, "We live insofar as we annihilate others, and the reparations or replacements we offer count for nothing. Might, then, the extinguishing of humanity—at our own hands and preferably without commotion—be the only 'good deed' that remains to us?"[40] Schirmacher refers to Hannah Arendt's concept of *Vita Activa* and her argument for the return to the Greeks of labouring, working, and acting. The ability to begin again, *to return*, is a human capacity—a *being-able-to-start* and not to fall into the *temptation of non-thought*. There is the human capacity for clearing a path to the side. In *The Human Condition*, Arendt argues that *animal laborans* and *homo faber* are juxtaposed to the life of action as the pinnacle of the modern inversion of the relation of *Vita Activa* and *Vita Contemplativa*. The human being is the cause of all this commotion according to Schirmacher, and since the human being cannot play God, the species must be fired for the good of all.[41] Inside the question of ecology is the assumption that the human animal should be saved along with Nature. Instead of accepting such an assumption, Schirmacher asks why should the human animal be saved at all? Why save humanity, let it die for the good of all! Who are human beings? They should really ask themselves – are they really worth caring for? Schirmacher suggests that forgetting about humanity, forgetting there are humans at all, might be the only way.

While facing-off with the aforementioned ecological 'assumption', Badiou proposes "tying being, truth and the subject to philosophy,"[42] as a move against nihilistic tendencies. He sees "the question of the subject who is in charge of finding the solution to the problem"[43] as embedded inside the question of Nature. Within the paradox is a challenge being proposed to find a solution to the existential threat imposed on the collective. Inside the question, for Badiou, "is a passion for absolute change which necessitates the destructive passion."[44] With the properly political problem of ecology already outlined, we can begin to see how Badiou's ontological framework of an epistemological break with both empiricism and idealism, has a radically different angle to contribute to the discussion. He proposes to move beyond the "statist fiction of the political,"[45] since essential to Badiou's reworking of the subject within the political, is the idea that the state cannot define the limits of the political field. Badiou argues, "every subject is political. This is why there are few subjects and rarely any politics."[46] For Badiou, the project of political change is the labour of producing new truths by a subject that maintains fidelity to the event:

> As a reopening of history, the event is heralded by three signs, all of them immanent in massive popular demonstrations: intensification, contraction and localization…with them begins the labour of the new truth which, in politics, is called 'organization.' An organization lies at the intersection between an Idea and an event.[47]

The seizure of truths is tested through truth's material experimentation in the world. The truth either is or it isn't, "the truth is not convivial or affective, because its power goes no farther than to be or not to be."[48] Bruno Bosteels, discussing Badiou's truth procedures, writes:

> truth in order to become effective in the situation, must be forced. That this is always the case should not be understood in the sense of a structural variant. *Forcing* is, on the contrary, that which in principle breaks, through a symptomatic and reflective torsion, with all structural transcendental points of view…the structure is supposed to include what we might call its point of internal excess, its constitutive outside. [49]

Badiou proposes to recover being, the subject, and truth from the ideology of democracy and human rights under the condition of late-capitalism. His work is also an attempt to seize truths by engaging with the real that has a relationship to the body of the subject, similar to Walter Benjamin. Badiou writes, "the real always ends up offering itself as an ordeal of the body,"[50] further arguing that a militant philosophy involves "a forceful occupation of the empty place."[51] *Forcing*, as such, produces an anticipatory knowledge of the new situation,[52] where the desire for true political change does not fall for the "traps of simulacrum, terror or disaster."[53] The event has infinite consequences; in its intensity, there is a visibility that is revealed even in its potential dissipation and contraction.

Badiou insists, "for what counts is not only the exceptional intensity of its surging up—the fact that we are dealing with a violent episode that creates appearing—but the glorious and uncertain consequences that this upsurge, despite its vanishing, sets out." [54]

Badiou makes a distinction between the identification of a given trace and what a trace means as movement in the world, writing: "it is not enough to identify a trace. One must incorporate into what the trace authorizes in terms of consequences."[55] All of these aspects of thinking political change are essential to understanding the question of ecology. In the formation of the subject and the seizing of truths is an active process of subjectivization, "if we understand that to participate, point by point, in the process of the creation of subjectivizable bodies is what renders life more powerful than survival."[56] As Lacan once said, "structures do not walk the streets."[57] Truths appear, in other words, through the subject to the event, rather than as universalizable structures or modes of being. Badiou argues that, "existence must be thought as the movement that goes from pure being to *being-there*,"[58] proposing that, "the Idea is the mediation between the individual and the Subject of a truth."[59] Again, he writes, "we must therefore accept that for the materialist dialectic, 'to live' and 'to live for an Idea' are one and the same thing."[60] In this sense, the movement from being to thing to subject must operate through the singularity of the event in order to reach *being-there*. This *being-there* is only possible through a fidelity to the event and the belief in an Idea, making possible the evasion of domination, capture, and a culture of inoperativity by the limited corporatist state form of politics or the matrix of control presented by capital flows.

Understanding the militant subject is essential to understanding the call for change presented by ecology today. Consider the example of the Paris Commune that momentarily opened up a rupture of the possible as a consequence of the failed revolution of 1848, of which Marx famously describes Bonaparte's coup as *a history without events.*[61] In such an event a commitment is called forth, one that may be described by Lacan's axiom, "do not give up on your desire."[62] This is not some sort of sacrificial condition for Badiou —it is a source of joy, he writes that to "live as a subject, to live for the Idea, is a source of happiness,"[63] even having referenced his own father's involvement in the French resistance as the happiest time in his life because he was living in the real as a result of a fidelity to the event. Living in the real is the unspeakable for Lacan, a trauma, whereas for Badiou, the real reflects the exceptional situation of the event and formation of the subject in the search of truth as a material labour, the movement from being to *being-there*. Fidelity to the event requires an incredible existential resilience that has a connection to the true Platonic life; for Badiou, the willingness "to keep going, then, presumes the ability to identify and resist the various forms of corruption or exhaustion that can beset a fidelity to truth."[64]

Philosophy and Event

What, then, can philosophy offer to the contemporary crisis of ecology? According to Badiou, "philosophy proposes a sorting procedure amid the confusion of experience, from which it draws an orientation. This elevation of confusion to orientation is the philosophical operation par excellence and its specific didactics."[65] Philosophy also produces truths in its own time, without suturing itself to its own conditions. It is an affirmative creation, a pure creation. Regarding philosophy, Badiou adds that "it's a diagnosis of the epoch: what does the epoch propose? It is a construction on the basis of this contemporary proposition of a concept of truth. And, finally, it's an existential experience relative to the true life."[66]

A politics must be constructed outside the false limits of the world proposed by the state and capital. That is why philosophy must work at a distance from power. Badiou's evental politics involve an act of fidelity both localized *and* universalizable, and of a scale that produces a change in the direction of the real, arguing that, "emancipatory politics…must be at least equal to the challenge of capital."[67] For him, "fidelity to the declaration is crucial, for truth is a process, and not an illumination,"[68] and this is where we witness the vital move from being to the subject. He writes, "what is at stake is nothing less than the possibility, for philosophy, to contribute to maintaining politics in the realm of the thinkable and to save the figure of being that politics detains, against the automatisms of the indifferent." [69]

The pure creation of a new modern tradition answerable to the question of ecology today, is contingent upon the event. The event is an immanent rupture in the world. It is a point where the normal laws of the world are not completely active. The event is more than a transformation, insofar as it is an exception to the general laws of the world. An event can be defined as an *immanent exception*. It must be internal to the situation as well as an exception to it. There is a tension between the inside of the situation that is in some sense reducible to the laws of the world itself. Secondly, there is a *localization* to the event within the situation, for the event is without any idea of totality. Localization is an important experimentation that occurs at the boundary between two different forms, where it is vital to be near the *limit point*. There are forms of being beside the situation between two determinations. Within it, is a determination to *exist*. The event is not the creation of something; it is the creation of *the possibility of something new to exist*, according to Badiou. The newness dwells within the potential consequences of this opening of a new possibility. [70]

The new *is* a consequence of what exists and also *appears* as a consequence of what exists. As an understanding of the opening of a new possibility, the subject asks the question, *does the world continue as it is*? The subject to the event asks, in concrete terms, *what is the new repetition that maintains fidelity to the event*? To realize the possibility of something new, it must be outside of determination and of absolute novelty. It could be argued that novelty today in ecology is a consequence of an event that opens up the true political space on the side of the continuation of Nature as a new modern tradition, and a repetition of the natural world in relation to human and animal existence through the militant work of a subject. It attempts to restore, through creative novelty and the repetition of a new modern tradition, a balanced metabolic interaction between humanity and Nature. Ecology is simultaneously a question of being today, and of *being-there*. It is in this situation that the dialectical contradiction between *the good life* and *suffering*, between *courage* and *anxiety*, unfolds.[71]

The most basic, yet most fundamental demands of Badiou are traced in his questions: what is politics and what is political action? And furthermore, what would constitute a *political event?* What is the *political localization* of an event, and what is its *limit point?* The boundary lies between the state and the subjective situation of the people. The state, obsessed with order by any means, enforces a formalization of the life of the people. For Badiou, "whenever there is a genuinely political event, the state reveals itself. It reveals its excess of power, its repressive dimension."[72] The formalization of the life of the people by the state is, of course, very different from the life of the people themselves according to Badiou. Real power, then, is the formalization of the life of the people themselves without the mediation of the state; a formalization motivated by a desire for an adequate self-representation of the people and their proper life. Power cannot be true power if it is too divorced from the true desire of the people.[73]

Badiou acknowledges the progressive desperation of the state in every epoch. The law is considered violent because of the determination that the state must continue. For Badiou, a law or an axiom which is formed from outside is a proof of the weakness of the state. He argues that the state is perceived as a necessity and the people that are inside the formalization of their life by the state do not openly revolt against that formalization. A political event, on the other hand, is the creation of a possibility in which the localized people affirm their conception of a proper life; it is the possibility of the people to affirm that they are different and irreducible to the state. As a true affirmation of the people, the mediation of this possibility is inside the people themselves, playing out as a fight between the true and the false from within. It is, according to Badiou, a *poetical* articulation of the true life against the false formalization of life mediated by the state. The event thereby opens up an operation of a new possibility considering the general affirmation of forms. The subject must be somebody without being on the inside, but must affirm one's existence from outside, generating the possibility of infinite consequences.[74]

We could argue that the destruction of the dinosaurs was an *ecological event* even though humanity did not yet exist. It was possibly an event without subjects. *Anthropogenic climate change* and the *Great Acceleration* (the rapid increase of climate impacts since the 1950s) today is something like an ecological event—something entirely new as a conception of what an event might be. The *ecological event* today is an absolute entanglement of humanity and Nature. The Anthropocene is possibly leading to the sixth mass extinction event in the history of the earth, but its causal condition is driven for the first time by the collective organization and effects of the human animal. The Anthropocene could also be a new truth in the field of science.

Political truths are inventions between individuals and the collective. They produce something universal, insofar as they exceed exchange between those individuals and the collective, but belong to everyone. The event is an opening of a possibility that affords novel access to the real, and is a material process as a consequence of such an exception. It escapes, in other words, the formalization of the field and the closure of the field by the laws of state and capital. In normal conditions of the world as it is, the state and capital prescribe what is *possible* and what is *impossible*, and the possibility of the real is reduced and excluded. According to Badiou's ontology, the state cannot authentically be a part of universality.

It is the task of philosophy to produce new truths and draw consequences from them. As a rupture with the world as it is, the emergence of a new possibility is constituted by the relationship between *exception* and *truth*. In Badiou's terms, it is the subject that affirms this new possibility and the work of philosophy to "inscribe in a new language something like the secret truth of the world, not the appearance of the world, but to force from the language something like a fragment, a trace, that not only a world exists but that it can name truths."[75]

Philosophy must also break with historicism, what Badiou character-izes as the "'museum' of philosophy, in favour a new materiality in order to seize truths with 'autonomous legitimation.'"[76] Badiou argues that, "philosophy must assume the axioms of thought and draw the conse-quences. It is only then, and starting from its immanent determination, that [philosophy] will convene its own history."[77]

For Badiou, (as well as for Jacques Rancière), true democracy is an exception that only exists from time to time, rather than a parliamentary structure. 'Democracy' is the name of an exceptional situation regard-ing the people, the *demos*. Badiou argues that true democracy is a pure opposition between mass democracy and state democracy, wherein true democracy moves from the event, to the affirmation, to access to politics outside the state and the eventual negation of this 'outside' access by the state. The state is always in the field of political action; it is in the space of the people - there is a relation between the *inside* and the *outside*. Badiou argues that the state is always inviting you inside, whereas the formation of subjectivity, of *being-there*, must be from outside, otherwise 'subjectivity' is formed from the perspective of the state. The subject, on the basis of the first movement of affirmation, subtracts statist subjec-tivity, withdrawing body and language from its participation from the political enclosures of democratic materialism.

In the logics of state and capital, to be somebody is to be inside the state and, therefore, a part of capitalism. Badiou proposes that the vision of humanity today is of capitalism under the law of finitude, and it is this repetition and circulation that is in need of interrogation and overcoming. Particularly, in capitalist subjectivity, humanity is reduced to self-interest-ed, rational animals, known as *homo economicus,* whose sole motivation is driven by competition for profit. In this logic, there cannot exist any other form of collective existence. The militant subject, by contrast, must affirm his or her existence from outside the state and capital to create a new definition of the real. The possibility to be something else as a consequence of the event, outside the logic of the state and capital, is the process of becoming a subject, of *being-there*, that Badiou calls *the new possibility*.[78]

The Subject

Badiou defines humanity as the capacity to become a subject to an event. It is accepting this possibility, from outside the state that allows for the becoming of the subject constituted by his/her capacity to be an active part of a new truth. Key to overcoming the state is to understand its contemporary form, which Badiou aptly names *democratic materialism, standing* in contrast to *materialist dialectics. Democratic materialism* is the (reductive) objectivization of bodies and languages by the state; but there are not just bodies and languages for Badiou; there are also supernumerary, universal truths. The production of truths cuts through the terror of the common ideology trapped by the democratic materialism of our actuality. A human being is truly living when he or she lives as an agent, moving from particularity to universality, from a singular world to a universal truth, and this movement is what Badiou names *materialist dialectics.* For Badiou, *being as one is not, therefore nothing is.* Nothing is the structure of the void. Void is the "proper name of being" that is "universally included" in all.[79]

Badiou writes:

> There are many repetitions in political activity, many false novelties, and many attempts that result in failure. To begin to examine the proposition of change we must have the knowledge of its history. This is also true for a revolt, strike, or protest. It is even true for a revolution. We must know the history of successes and failures. We must know why certain political actions do not provide us with a good result, and so on. We cannot have a purely new consciousness without memory.[80]

Though he argues that philosophy should develop axioms and draw consequences from them in order to not be enslaved to the history of philosophy, he does acknowledge that thinking change requires knowledge of the history of change. Badiou argues that the call for emergency in the question of ecology is similar to the *passion for the real* of the last century, again making the distinction between a subject who is under the conditions of an event with that of the "Leninist idea that change is under the condition of a new Subject."[81] With the omnipotent status of the subject without fidelity to an event, Badiou argues that there emerges the possibility of disaster.

The Death of God and a New Relation to Human Death

A new historical vision of Nature can also be viewed as a new meditation on death, according to Badiou, since "nature is the most important serial killer, it is without comparison."[82] This particular relation to death indicates something beyond the religious idea of death that Badiou refers to as an old idea of death. Badiou places this question of ecology, through Nietzsche and Foucault, as being inside of the consequences of the philosophical axiom of the *death of God*. Badiou argues that "capitalism is the consequence of the death of God and not the solution to the problem opened up by the death of God."[83] The twentieth-century legacy is of humanity placing itself in the role of God, that is a legacy of the deification of capital and the human interpellation of capitalism's regulative and moral order. The human being may be dead and "capital," as Robin Mackay and Armen Avenessia write, "has become independent of human will."[84] Humanity responds to the crisis with its fundamental phantasm, which, to borrow one of Slavoj Žižek's insights, is ideology at the political level.

For Giorgio Agamben, the features of democratic order comes in the form of a command:

> These days, the words "crisis" and "economy" are not used as concepts but rather as words of command that facilitate the imposition and acceptance of measures and restrictions that the people would not

otherwise accept. Today, "crisis" means, "you must obey!" I think it is very obvious to everyone that the so-called "crisis" has been going on for decades and that it is actually nothing but the normal functioning of capitalism in our time. And there is nothing rational about the way capitalism is now functioning…In order to understand what is taking place, we have to interpret Walter Benjamin's idea that capitalism is really a religion literally, the most fierce, implacable and irrational religion that has ever existed because it recognizes neither truces nor redemption. A permanent worship is celebrated in its name, a worship whose liturgy is labor and its object, money. God did not die; he was transformed into money.[85]

Inscribed within the question of ecology today is the real possibility of historically unprecedented climate catastrophes in the near future, within our lifetime, and across the world. This existential crisis will be a collectively- and individually-embodied experience conducted at multiple speeds and intensities over time, with the likelihood of localizable, asymmetrical effects. Climate crises propose a challenge not just to a form of human living, but to what it means to *be* human, forcing humanity to relearn how to experience the techniques of living within this accelerated state of permanent flux. Such crises also require a rethinking of the scale of change that is proposed, if humanity and Nature continue their current metabolic process *as it is*. In light of these crises, to overturn the world at a planetary scale and overcome the apparatus of capital and the state, the subject can only emerge as a consequence of, in this case, an *ecological event*. Such an event will ultimately be an ordeal of the body as a confrontation aiming to transcend both the life and death drive brought on by the problem of the Anthropocene. Badiou writes:

ultimately life is the wager, made on a body that has entered into appearing, that one will faithfully entrust this body with a new temporality, keeping at a distance the conservative drive (the ill named 'life' instinct) as well as the mortifying drive (the death instinct). Life is what gets the better of the drives…Because it prevails over the drives, life engages in the sequential creation of a present, and this creation both constitutes and absorbs a new type of past.[86]

The problem of ecology and the possibility of collective finitude today is unique and singular in terms of its specificity. But it is not a new phenomenon in that the concern with collective finitude has occurred as a consistent theme of human existence historically; each epoch, that is, has its own relation to impending catastrophes and the challenge presented by surpassing disasters. Within the movement of ecology, however, is also a theoretical intervention – ultimately, an attempt to understand today what properly philosophical questions are embedded within the conditions posed by the dialectical relation and metabolic interaction between humanity and Nature, and its excess.

The consequences of the problems opened up by this relation between humanity and Nature recall the complexity of Timothy Morton's notion of hyperobjects such as geological time scales, the possibilities of civilizational collapse, and the spectre of species extinction, including that of humanity. Through the consideration of the paradox of ecology is the contemporary renovation of the philosophical question of being itself. As a consequence, there are ramifications to the ordering of other worlds including aesthetic regimes, the relation between order and justice, a reorganization of the categories of Truth, Beauty, Justice, the Good Life, Politics, Love, and so on. As one writer ruminates, "What does my life mean in the face of death?...What does one life mean in terms of species death?"[87] Within these questions is the possibility of learning to die as a collective rather than as individuals. There is also the death of narrative in the being towards death and in the connection between the living world and the underworld.

French writer Michel de Montaigne, in paraphrasing the words of Cicero, thought that studying philosophy was akin to learning how to die. In many writings in philosophy, death is considered to be a part of the natural world, and the coming to terms with it to be a part of life—the thing that gives life its very meaning. "If you don't know how to die," Montaigne wrote, don't worry; "Nature will tell you what to do on the spot, fully and adequately."[88] Michael Taussig theorizes about the re-enchantment of the Sun in the Age of Global Meltdown. The expenditure and exchange of cosmic energy by the Sun is a source of life and a source of death. This was the world of many cultures not very long ago. Our collective dialectical relation to the Sun is inside the question of ecology today.

Ecology gives us a new conception of death rather than a traditional, historical vision of death, which is really a religious vision of death. The death of God proposes a new relation to death, according to Badiou, which points to the future possibility of collective death not only for humanity but for other living species as well. Imagining the end of the world itself is thus in the realm of the thinkable. This is perhaps not a new purpose for philosophy; it is indeed what was posed as a possibility by the expansion of the arms race and the threat of nuclear war in the twentieth century following the Second World War. Within that question was the idea that nuclear war was a human choice that could be averted through negotiation. Within our time however, there is also the idea of collective death, beyond a human-induced possibility: comets or asteroids could just as easily destroy the world in the future, and it would have nothing to do with the hubris and stupidity of the human animal. Ecology, in particular challenges us to think beyond our own time and demonstrate a duty to care for the present and the future, and to build a relation to those not yet living. Within that challenge is the call to make sacrifices today not only against a way of living that supports the contemporary capitalist form itself, but as part of the responsibility to build an affirmative project that harmonizes the metabolic disorder between humanity and Nature as a consequence of the event. For Albert Camus, choosing to live or die was the ultimate philosophical question, as he writes in the The Myth of Sisyphus, "There is only one really serious philosophical problem and that is suicide. Deciding whether or not life is worth living is to answer the fundamental question in philosophy. All other questions follow from that."[89] Ecology demands of us a resistance to the world as it is through the affirmation of the new possibility for the forcing of the true life for the purposes of preservation.

Inside the question of ecology is a meditation on death. There is an acknowledgement that Nature can destroy humankind, just as humankind can destroy the landscapes and living beings inside of Nature. Badiou argues that, inscribed within the problem of ecology "is an invention of a non-religious question of death."[90] He argues that inside the question of ecology is a call, for not a change *inside* the modern world but a *change of* the modern world itself; it is the desire to find an outside. If the modern world today is an affirmation of the disjunction between history and Nature, it is a call for *a new modern tradition*. He writes, "if we want to modify the relationship between history and nature we must modify our relationship also to death." [91] Within the question of ecology is the immanent relation between humankind and Nature. Within this, is also a new idea concerning life and death, history and Nature.

The appearing and becoming of a true life requires submission to a truth process in the real rather than to judgment, as part of a materialist dialectics. Truth is a relation to what is happening, whereas judgment is only a repetition. To affirm its novelty, Badiou insists, the truth must be submitted to chance: at some point a wager is made that the event has taken place. Without the ability to calculate or verify this, a decision is made to maintain fidelity to that wager. But, of course, forcing the limit point can be a site of disaster. For Badiou, the truth procedure can only be adjudicated outside the rules of established knowledge, and is not reducible to the individual. It is, rather, an affirmation of the collective possibility of the world as such. The truth is infinite and certainly beyond any notion of finitude.[92] For Lacan, overcoming the death drive is the beginning of desire. [93]

As was mentioned earlier in the chapter, what ultimately separates Badiou from Lenin's thought is this idea of the *irreducibility of the subject*, in relation to the event as such. In particular, the idea that the subject emerges as a consequence of the event and is actualized in this fidelity to it, for Badiou, and it is not the subject who creates the event as it is for Lenin.

On Mourning

The possibility of an affirmative political project is always limited by the conditions from which it originates. What is counted and what is not counted, by whom and for whom, are necessary questions. As Judith Butler writes:

> To decide what views will count as reasonable within the public domain, however, is to decide what will and will not count as the public sphere of debate. And if someone holds views that are not in line with the nationalist norm, that person comes to lack credibility as a speaking person, and the media is not open to him or her...The foreclosure of critique empties the public domain of debate and democratic contestation itself, so that debate becomes the exchange of views among the like-minded, and criticism, which ought to be central to any democracy, becomes a fugitive and suspect activity. [94]

The question of ecology and crisis today is also tied into the labour that comes with mourning. As Butler continues,

> one mourns when one accepts that by the loss one undergoes one will be changed, possibly forever. Perhaps mourning has to do with agreeing to undergo a transformation (perhaps one should say *submitting* to a transformation) the full result of which one cannot know in advance.[95]

There is an accounting and accepting of what is possible to grieve:

> Some lives are grievable and others are not; the differential allocation of grievability that decides what kind of subject is and must be grieved, and which kind of subject must not operates to produce and maintain certain exclusionary conceptions of what counts as a livable life and a grievable death.[96]

There are bodies that do not matter and have been extinguished from the public sphere as being mournable. Ashlee Cunsolo Willox extends Judith Butler's argument to non-human bodies, arguing that animals, vegetables, and minerals need to be brought in to the realm of the grievable. These bodies "cannot be mourned because they are always already lost or, rather, never were."[97] Willox also raises a possibility of an *anticipatory* mourning for losses yet to come, or a *place-based mourning* about a changing landscape. She argues that, "we need…mechanisms that can extend grievability to non-human bodies and recognize them as mournable subjects, particularly within discourses of climate change."[98] The being-towards-death is a fact of life—our finite existence places its own limits *a priori*. Mourning begins with the other's death while we are still alive, as such; mourning is the work of the living. Butler argues that true mourning arrives when one submits to the possibility of *transformation*. In mourning, we "not only lose something that was loved, but we also lose our former selves, the way we used to be before the loss."[99]

We are called to engage with the responsibility posed by death—"a call to responsibility to engage with what was lost."[100] What are the deaths we disavow if we can overcome an Anthropocentric notion of mourning? Willox argues, through Derrida, "there is no politics without an organization of the time and space of mourning."[101] It is in this capacity for shared suffering, the real lived experience of collective trauma, that the event can be called forth. Dying forces upon us a calling to speak in order to break the silence. As Derrida writes, "speaking is impossible but so too would be silence or absence or a refusal to share one's sadness."[102] Mourning, to be done well, must therefore ultimately fail in its act. Inscribed in each death is the death of a world, "suggesting that the end of the world can come more than once."[103] Derrida writes of *posthumous infidelity*—when a friend dies and another's life goes on,[104] wherein the possibility of collective finitude invokes the possible erasure of worlds, friendships, and relations. It is possible to mourn that which is not dead, Derrida adds, as a kind of *anticipatory mourning*.[105] This is what the question of Nature magnifies and disorients through its relation to global warming as a *hyperobject*. As Derrida writes:

> To have a friend, to look at him, to follow him with your eyes, to admire him in friendship, is to know in a more intense way, already injured, always insistent, and more and more unforgettable, that one of the two of you will inevitably see the other die. One of us, each says to himself, the day will come when one of the two of us will see himself

no longer seeing the other and so will carry the other within him a while longer, his eyes following without seeing, the world suspended by some unique tear, each time unique, through which everything from then on, through which the world itself—and this day will come—will come to be reflected quivering, reflecting disappearance itself: the world, the whole world, the world itself, for death takes us from us not only some particular life within the world, some moment that belongs to us, but, each time, without limit, someone through whom the world, and first of all our own world, will have opened up in a both finite and infinite—mortally infinite—way. That is the blurred and transparent testimony borne by this tear, this small, infinitely small, tear, which the mourning of friends passes through and endures even before death, and always singularly so, always irreplaceably.[106]

For Kierkegaard, to be in a state of melancholy was something like a journey to a holy experience—it was the sickness that you must go through to be holy.[107] But, in ecology today there remains a kind of narcissism of the suffering human body, the animals, and the natural world. The problem of mourning, as it relates to ecology, is that it persists in functioning within the spiral of existential finitude, rather than engaging with ecology as a human construction that can properly negotiate the possibility of a future world beyond finitude. Is there the possibility that learning to mourn in a new way can move a human being closer to becoming a subject of change? For Badiou, the human being, as a subject, cannot exist without resistance as a part of being. In some sense, there is mourning for the inability to bring about a utopian project. There is a desire for *releasement,* an action against action, a desire for a way out. In *ekstasis,* the will to will, there is the tension between earth and worlds. With technology as a form of mediation, it also reduces the way being reveals itself.

Žižek, in *Living in the End Times*, discusses how our collective social consciousness comes to grips with the potential of a coming apocalypse:

The first reaction is one of ideological denial: there is no fundamental disorder; the second is exemplified by explosions of anger at the injustices of the new world order; the third involves attempts at bargaining ("if we change things here and there, life could perhaps go an as before"); when the bargaining fails, depression and withdrawal set in; finally, after passing through this zero-point, the subject no longer perceives the situation as a threat, but as the chance of a new beginning—or as Mao Zedong put it: "There is great disorder under heaven, the situation is excellent."[108]

Morton argues that many arguments around ecology suffer from Hegel's *Beautiful Soul* syndrome. The desire for Gaia reduces the possibility of the subject of change and Nature remains an object *over there*. He writes:

> The landscape on the other side of the chasm between subject and object turns out to be the beautiful soul in inverted form. We could call it "beautiful Nature." It suffers from the same elements as the beautiful soul: it is opaque, exclusionary, absolutely right and proper…the beautiful soul beats its heart against a solid wall. Nature remains a reified object, "over there."[109]

For Adorno, there is an encounter with non-identity in the void of Nature. Ecology ultimately is a movement from *being* to *being-with*. But we are living today in a world where, according to Morton, the Catastrophe has already taken place. It is a world in which "the problems are initiated by scales of capital and the risk becomes democratic."[110] The Catastrophe brings into appearance the poetics of the unknown danger and the annihilation of space by time. With the surpassing disaster, there is the opening to utopias/dystopias beyond our reckoning.

What is Ecology as Such Today?

Ecology, in its call for thinking the future, also demands an interrogation of the *here and now* to adequately bring about change in the future. Ecology is not an abstract, imaginary thing; it compels us to ask what are we going to do now as a propositional change in the relationship between humanity and Nature? Ecology, in its traditional form, comes from *oecol-*

ogy, the area of science dealing with living things and their environment. The etymology originates from the Greek *oikos,* or house, dwelling or place of habitation, and, *logia,* or study of, and began to pick up use in the 1960's in relation to pollution activities. I am proposing a new usage of 'ecology' as it relates to the movement of creating a fundamental change in the relationship between humanity and Nature towards the continuation of existence as such.

'Climate' comes from the Greek *klima* – zone or region, or literally to slope or to lean; similarly it's Latin derivative points to the same meaning. We are also concerned here with the production of social reorganization that lies within the question of ecology. In this sense, ecology cannot be the first problem; it is a general formalization of the very nature of politics, social in its formation, the movement from the one to the all, relating to ecology that fits within *metapolitics* - a vision of politics inside of philosophy. Ecology has a critical relationship to the modern world, imbued with the desire to transform the world as a formalization of a new relationship between humanity and Nature. This proposition forms the foundation of the metapolitics of ecology; it is a means of thinking the politics of ecology as a movement of change. Having framed ecology as a properly political question inside the subject, the coming task for contemporary philosophy is to determine the properly philosophical problems such a nested relation initiates. Ecology, in its relation to philosophy, asks: *can global warming be thought?*

Ecology, then, is an affirmative project concerned with the resurrection of Nature from its own deathbed. It is an attempt to rebalance the metabolic interaction between humanity and Nature beyond the political enclosures of the present and future presented by the state and capital. The traditional revolution is not a circle that displaces the old Master with a new Master, just as ecology is not the desire of humanity for Nature to be the new God or the solution to the problem opened up by the "death of God." For Badiou, true desire is always the desire for a monster, and for Lacan, there is no nastier Master than the one emerging from revolution. In ecology, we find the desire for a subjective emergence outside of a Master.

Ecology is an affirmative project of political invention as a novel formalization *between living beings and Nature*. Ecology seeks to bring about a new sequential repetition of the dialectical relation between history and Nature, as part of a new modern tradition. In contrast to the *passion for the real* of the last century and the consequences of such a disaster, ecology is the affirmatively militant project of changing the repetition of the world *as it is*, towards a repetition on the side of the continuation of Nature and its beings (human and other living things). It is a forceful attempt, through political novelty, to continue the existence of the collective as such, constituted within the world of change that situates humanity as a part of Nature, not apart from it. It calls for a new relation between humanity and science. It recognizes the singularity of the human species in its capacity to destroy the planet, and for the capacity of Nature to destroy humanity and the world of living and non-living beings. To think through ecology philosophically, it is vital to use the conditions of politics, love, science, and art that Badiou proposes as the truth conditions of philosophy to avert the disaster of suturing philosophy to one of its conditions. Through Badiou's work, *Ecological Metapolitics,* is *the consequences a philosophy is capable of drawing from the real instances of the project of ecology as thought. Ecological Metapolitics proposes for philosophy an ontology that thinks the possibilities of ecological political change from the perspective of the subject, in a movement towards the preservation of the natural world and existence as such.*

2

ECOLOGICAL METAPOLITICS:
A Case Against Democratic Materialism

Badiou and Democratic Materialism

Badiou is often thought of as a figure that constructs philosophical space in a heavy-handed way, but it is precisely because of his systemic invention for philosophy that we have at hand, a useful clearing procedure for thinking the movement of politics from the *impossible* to the *possible*. Badiou himself addresses charges of philosophical militancy in his thinking by arguing that, "theoretical anti-humanism can serve practical humanism, [in] that the most uncompromising scientific rationalism is compatible with the most unconditional assertion of collective human capacity."[111] Since for Badiou, philosophical truth procedures are only possible in light of events generated by politics, love, art and science, let us, firstly, clear some *philosophical debris*.

While Badiou says that we can protect these names—political philosophy, ethics, democracy, human rights—they must be defined *outside of the state* and made real in terms of their true meaning. Without such redefinition, he argues, they act as little more than ideological fixtures that stand in the way of substantive emancipatory change. Badiou provides a critique of liberal democracy by elaborating its tendency to depoliticize and immobilize thought and action. As he argues in his book *Ethics*:

> that these intellectual tendencies were at best variations on ancient
> religious and moral preaching, at worst a threatening mix of conserva-
> tism and the death drive…in that current of opinion which incessantly
> evokes "ethics," a severe symptom of renunciation of the one thing that

distinguishes the human species from the predatory living organism that it also is: the capacity to enter into the composition and becoming of some eternal truths.[112]

Badiou's work, including his *Manifesto for Philosophy* and *Metapolitics*, places his approach to philosophy in clear opposition to most definitions of, and liberal tendencies of, political philosophy, environmental ethics, democracy, and human rights circulating today. Broadly speaking, the 'morally' infused line of argumentation prevalent in the field of environmental ethics, finds a critical counter-position in Badiou's *Ethics*. It is my assertion, through Badiou, that definitions of political philosophy, environmental ethics, democracy, and human rights are too contaminated to effectively consider the paradox of the ecological question today. To think ecology philosophically, I will argue, we must recover these terms from their current usage in order to construct an affirmative definition for *Ecological Metapolitics*.

Badiou defines 'metapolitics' as,

whatever consequences a philosophy is capable of drawing, both in and for itself, from real instances of politics as thought. Metapolitics is opposed to political philosophy, which claims that since no such politics exists, it falls to philosophers to think 'the' political.[113]

A definition of *Ecological Metapolitics* will attempt to do the same for the question of ecology without embracing the theoretical excesses and hyperbole of movements like *deep ecology*. Badiou defines current and popular notions of political philosophy as a program that "accords philosophy the task of thinking it."[114] He argues that this position is problematic on a number of fronts and that it must be the task of philosophy to destroy the current limits placed upon the thinking of politics in the field of political philosophy. For Badiou, such a limited understanding of what constitutes political philosophy merely generates an analysis of the political and has a tendency to submit this limited view to ethical norms. In this formulation, the philosopher is merely "the analyst and thinker of this…objectivity…the one who determines the principles of good politics, of politics conforming to ethical demands…the one exempt from militant involvement in any genuine political process." [115]

For Badiou, democratic materialism,

> presents as an objective given, as result of historical experience, what it calls "the end of ideologies." What actually lies behind this violent subjective injunction whose real content is 'Live without Idea'…
> We are told this is the price to be paid for tolerance and respect of the Other. But each and every day we see that this tolerance is itself just another fanaticism, because it only tolerates its own vacuity…Contemporary skepticism…merely conforms to the rhetoric of instants and the politics of opinion…That is why democratic materialism in fact seeks to destroy what is external to it…it is a violent and warmongering ideology. [116]

> Metapolitics, and in this case *Ecological Metapolitics*, attempt to leap beyond the false enclosures of democratic materialism to rethink the politics of ecology in a radically deconsecrated realm – ultimately, to help create an outside for thinking militant political change topologically, regarding the question of ecology today.

Political Philosophy

In Badiou's breakdown, political philosophy ranks as little more than opinion and suffers from a distorted history that is a derivative byproduct of democratic materialism. He argues that a politics and philosophy defined from the perspective of the state is nothing more than sophistry. In his assessment 'political philosophy' turns politics into a passive commentary on public affairs, masking the defense of *a* politics. [117] Politics cannot be reduced to a consensual vision, [118] it must allow for the novel formation of a collective and the possibility for affirmative radical invention. In political philosophy, it is the spectators who define the rules of politics that police its limit point according to him. Badiou argues, moreover, that,

> a politics is hazardous, militant and always partially undivided fidelity

to evental singularity under a solely self-authorizing prescription. The universality of political truth that results from such a fidelity is itself legible, like all truth, only retroactively, in the form of a knowledge. Of course, the point from which a politics can be thought—which permits, even after the event, the seizure of its truth—is that of its actors, and not its spectators.[119]

In opposition to political philosophy, Badiou argues that "placing philosophy under the condition of emancipatory politics [...] requires us to begin from the beginning, from the recognition that politics itself is, in its being, in its doing, a thought."[120] Metapolitics refuses political philosophy's claims to "neutrality and critical reflection" and distinctly does not attempt to "seek ideological immunity for itself."[121] Jason Barker argues that, "against political philosophy, metapolitics seeks to politicize, beyond the limits of political theory, philosophical practice."[122] Importantly, Badiou's formulation of metapolitics is distinct from Louis Althusser's notion of theory being the class struggle in philosophy, referring to Althusser's intervention as an example of philosophy suturing itself to one of its conditions (politics) that ultimately results in a disaster for philosophy.

Badiou argues for a tactical withdrawal from the machinery of state politics in favor of a "politics without party"—a Maoist idea. Real politics emerges by subtracting itself from the symbolic fiction of the state apparatus; its limited (and limiting) definition of the political – now fully at the mercy of capital. Similar to Antonio Gramsci's notion of the organic intellectual, Badiou's idea of political intelligence comes from within the situation, but his *politics without a party* comes with a provision that emancipatory politics must affirm this "without lapsing into the figure of anarchism."[123] For Badiou, this reinforces the view of the state as a *representative constitutive fiction*[124] whose repressive force is revealed whenever there is a political event.[125]

In this sense, Badiou's idea of metapolitics is quintessentially a Platonic idea of thinking the political through philosophy. Badiou clearly defines philosophy as "a militant discourse on truth" and as a means of "seizing truths."[126] In keeping with Badiou's mathematical ontology, "truth is the void object = x of philosophy which follows in the wake of what is profoundly indiscernible for the subject and goes by the name of the event."[127] Badiou's idea of truth comes from Lacan in the sense that it comes after the event;[128] where we cannot ever know the real, but we are also never immobilized or paralyzed by the situation. There is always the possibility of affirmative construction.

For Badiou, philosophy should not present itself as a situation of truth, but rather as a *seizure* of truth.[129] His approach is a philosophical move from logic to ontology. When philosophy sutures itself to one of its conditions, what Badiou defines as a disaster for philosophy, it results in a reduction of thought that has the triple effect of turning truth *ecstatic, sacred,* or *terroristic.*[130]

Philosophy, furthermore, should not be beholden to its own history. Badiou argues that philosophy is "paralyzed by its relation to its own history,"[131] requiring it to engage in a kind of *suspended amnesia* with its own history if it is going to be available for the seizure of truths. Philosophy must develop axioms of thinking and draw consequences from them prior to placing them historically within the field of philosophy.[132] This is not Hegel's "end of history" but a break with the practice of historicism, albeit with conditions; those conditions being a militant relationship to truth. As such, Badiou argues that:

> philosophy is something like a logical revolt. Philosophy pits thought against injustice, against the defective state of the world and of life. Yet it pits thought against injustice in a movement which conserves and defends argument and reason, and which ultimately proposes a new logic.[133]

Badiou's philosophical project is about constructing a new present by subtracting the subject from the dominant order of capitalism and the state. In his formulation, "if philosophy is to be something in life, to be a way of life, as its very foundation attests it does and must, then, that it is today other than an academic quibble. The world must be turned upside down, 'existence changed', a present once again constituted."[134] The seizure of a truth is connected to the materiality of universalism in its movement from being to truth. In his book on St. Paul, Badiou proposes that, "the subjective process of a truth is one and the same thing as the love of that truth. And the militant real of that love is the universal address of what constitutes it. The materiality of universalism is the militant dimension of every truth."[135] Political philosophy and environmental ethics are academic disciplines that possess a certain normativity in their practices, limiting definitions of what constitutes the political and the ethical on the contemporary issue of global warming. These disciplines, as *disciplines*, offer little to the question of actual ecological change in the material world. For Badiou, "philosophy is always at risk of being betrayed by the Academies developed to transmit it," and demands that "Philosophy must tie the concept to life, to the real lives of subjects." [136] This idea of a living and circulating philosophy has the possibility of concrete consequences in public life.

Badiou's philosophy makes a decisive cut from empiricism and idealism, a binary he identifies as a relic of Enlightenment thinking. In this sense, philosophy has an antagonistic relation to the popular categories of political philosophy, environmental ethics, democracy, and human rights. Badiou's project deems political philosophy, for instance, to be not only a form of democratic materialism, but "the principle ideological obstacle to a politics of truth."[137] Philosophy is thus tasked with a mode of resistance against academic political philosophy and capital-parliamentarism.[138] Badiou further argues that, "policing politics in the name of human rights and ethics, is in essence the denial that politics has anything to do with thought and truth."[139] Since politics proper happens at a distance from the state, a subtractive ontology must be deployed for a philosophical procedure that summons lack and brings forth "the Idea."[140]

By beginning as a subtraction from the definitions inscribed by the state in a particular situation, the truth begins as a singularity, yet has the capacity for universal address. The truth is universal-singular; it is a material construction and involves *being true* as an act of fidelity to an eventual rupture. Ethics, bound to democratic materialism, largely play a regulative function in policing the parameters of the acceptable limit point of state-sanctioned conceptions of political possibility and political time.

Additionally, from Badiou's perspective, "all ethical predication based on recognition of the other should be purely and simply abandoned."[141] Whatever *ought* to be, should be valid for all. Ethics, for Badiou, are situation-specific behaviors indifferent to differences[142] in notable contradistinction to thinkers like Levinas' whose ethics of the other, Badiou has positioned as anti-philosophy. A truth is something that happens particularly to you, but that can also be universalizable. Badiou writes:

> As a general rule, every generic procedure is in reality a process that can perfectly well be deliberative, as long as we understand that *it invents its rule of deliberation at the same time as it invents itself*. And it is no more constrained by a pre-established norm that follows from the rule of deliberation. You have only to look at how the rule of deliberation in different organizations, in different political sequences, and in different political modes, is entirely variable…Every time a plurality of individuals, a plurality of human subjects, is engaged in a process of truth, the construction of this process induces the construction of a deliberative and collective figure of this production, which is itself variable.[143]

In making this argument, Badiou jettisons postmodernism's conception of *otherness* as a formative basis for ethics. In calling for the singular situation to have the capacity for universalism, Badiou is closer to Hegel in his conception of ethics, insofar as Hegel draws a distinction between ethics (*Sittlichkeit*) as immediate action, and morality (*Moralität*) as reflexive action.[144]

Ecological Metapolitics and Democratic Materialism

Ecological Metapolitics calls forth the invention of a new modern tradition for ecology, premised on the philosophical rejection of contemporary uses of the terms political philosophy, environmental ethics, democracy, and human rights rooted in democratic materialism. The world exists as it does *because* of these terms, placing a hold on the past, constructing norms that limit the fields of political action in the present, as well as potential movements towards the future. Democratic materialism, as I argue through Badiou's work, is a morally regulated system that polices acceptable discourse from the perspective of the state and capital, on the side of the repetition of the capitalist world *as it is.*

Similarly, Peter Sloterdijk has argued:

> the "age of extremes" seems to be over—passed like a spook, that, in retrospect, no one any longer understands what made it powerful. Radicalism is only important in the Western Hemisphere as an aesthetic attitude, perhaps also as philosophical habitus, but no longer as a political style. The center, the most formless of monsters, consistently understood the law of the hour. It made itself into the protagonist, even solo entertainer on the post-historical stage. Whatever it touches becomes, just like itself, docile, characterless, and despotic. Yesterday's agents of extremist impatience have become unemployed and are no longer offered any parts to play in the zeitgeist. What is called for now are resilient bores. What is expected of them is to sit around big tables to come up with the world formula of compromise. The relentlessly soft center creates hybrids out of everything. [145]

The movement from *being* to *subject* is essential to the question of ecology today. Badiou proposes the "necessity of the question of being to the renovation of philosophy."[146] He argues that philosophy should act in its own name and "institute a regime of discourse which is its own earthly legitimation."[147] In *Theory of the Subject*, he defines courage as "insubordination to the symbolic order at the urging of the dissolutive injunction of the real."[148] Badiou calls for a just audacity of recomposition, arguing that the dominant class closely manages the repetition of the world as it is.[149] Badiou contends that true political action is a struggle of the true against the false,[150] where 'political philosophy' is nothing more than the propaganda that "the state must endlessly retain a monopoly on the definition of political time."[151]

To think through *Ecological Metapolitics* as a "forceful occupation of the empty place,"[152] which requires the necessary subtraction from the state and the logic of capital, the movement must become a basis for a new repetition of an affirmative political project, as the construction of thought. Badiou adds that "the essence of politics is not the plurality of opinions…it requires us to begin from the beginning, from the recognition that politics itself is, in its being, in its doing, a thought."[153] In Badiou's work, there is a distinction between truth and knowledge: truth is the material labor that always cuts a hole through knowledge. By critiquing the popular definitions of political philosophy, environmental ethics, democracy, and human rights as the gatekeepers of the contemporary question of ecology, philosophy, as envisioned through Badiou's ontology, can allow us to think more openly about the principle of *forcing*, which "produces an anticipatory knowledge of the new situation."[154]

Badiou argues that, "in order to think the contemporary world in any fundamental way, it's necessary to take as your point of departure not the critique of capitalism but the critique of democracy. To separate thought, from the dominant forms of ideology, has always been one of philosophy's crucial tasks…how does it operate as a subjective fetish."[155] For Badiou, there is a disconnect between political invention and the obstructionary role played by the neo-liberal state and its instrumentalized usage of terms, such as democracy, human rights, and ethics to police the limit point of what constitutes political possibility. Badiou writes:

> The real question is that of an affirmative proposition regarding democracy, as something other than the consensus on the parliamentary form of politics. This is what the paradox that you point to tries to conceal, in other words, that the truly risky philosophical imperative, the one that really poses problems for thought, is the critique of the democratic form as we know it.[156]

Political philosophy is too close to state power for Badiou to have a genuine relationship to truth. The rationality of the state has been used to distort the true possibilities of political philosophy for him. He writes, it is the use of the State's model of managerial rationality as a grid for the speculative understanding of history that establishes the historico-political continuum. And that continuum now makes it possible to use the same vocabulary and the same grid of intelligibility to speak of history and to analyze the management of the State.[157]

Environmental Ethics and Philosophy

Regarding the question of ecology, environmental ethics, too often, places moral responsibility on to the individual and develops a discourse that circulates widely in the academy, the media sphere and advocacy organizations alike. Campaigns that rely on environmental ethics in practice, however, rarely function on, or respond to, the scale of capital. Environmental ethics become subsumed within contemporary culture's reductive issues of recycling, carbon credits, bike lanes, carbon footprints, bin buddies, sustainable business practices, and other feel-good local interventions rather than attending to the demands of full-scale systemic change; too often functioning within the bounds of capital circulation.

Badiou argues that ethics in the Western sense merely perform a regulative function and that philosophy should therefore repudiate the conventional form of the good.[158] Through Foucault, Althusser, and Lacan, Badiou critiques the contemporary use of ethics, suggesting that politics has been subordinated to ethics and the "judgment of the spectator."[159] Susan Sontag, who writes about the ethics of photography and aesthetics, critiques normative understandings of ethics in this way:

> To designate a hell is not, of course, to tell us anything about how to extract people from that hell, how to moderate hell's flames. Still, it seems a good in itself to acknowledge, to have enlarged, one's sense of how much suffering caused by human wickedness there is in the world we share with others. Someone who is perennially surprised that depravity exists, who continues to feel disillusioned (even incredulous) when confronted with evidence of what humans are capable of inflicting in the way of gruesome, hands-on cruelties upon other humans, has not reached moral or psychological adulthood...No one after a certain

age has the right to this kind of innocence, of superficiality, to this degree of ignorance, or amnesia.[160]

It is Badiou's contention that the conventional use of ethics stands on the side of *democratic materialism* along with received notions of human rights, state democracy, and the contemporary consensus of the common ideology. Badiou's critique of the contemporary use of the word "ethics" argues that the language has been largely stripped of meaning and has too often led to the denial of thinking,[161] leading him to propose a definition of ethics that stands outside of democratic materialism.

Ecological Metapolitics as Affirmative Construction

If philosophy's task is to reconstitute an outside through an affirmative dialectic, can it provide an account of the event that is plausible? The Paris Commune emerges within the context of the Franco-Prussian War that exacerbates the social contradictions within French society. It could be argued that such negation is what transforms impossibility into possibility: the appearance of the people as a subject. It must also, equally, be asserted, that this possibility does not drop from the sky. [162] Badiou argues that although we must begin a new political sequence through affirmative dialectics, negation is still necessary for philosophical construction. But given the *passion for the real* of the last century, we can create with less negation than before. For Badiou, to keep going then "presumes the ability to identify and resist various forms of corruption and exhaustion that can beset a fidelity to truth."[163] Badiou wagers that "philosophy's duty is clear: to reconstitute rationally the infinite reserve of the affirmative that every liberating project requires…[P]hilosophy is the attic where, in difficult times, one accumulates resources, lines up tools and sharpens knives."[164]

Philosophy must be an affirmative invention toward truth and the real. Futhermore, Badiou warns against a messianic millenarianism with the contemporary ecology movement, arguing instead for a movement that can functionally resist at the scale of capital. In his sense of what must be done, he writes, "we have to destroy capital's domination, extricate ourselves from its democratic propaganda, and concentrate our already extremely limited forces on this point, rather than making deals with green banks on account of the climate."[165] Badiou views philosophy's role as one of corrupting the youth in the sense of Socrates—that is, "to convey the means by which they can avoid being subjugated to prevailing opinions."[166] His definition of philosophy is best understood in his own words:

> that singular discipline of thought that has [as] its departure point the conviction that there are truths. From there, it is led towards an imperative, a vision of life…that which has value for human individuals, that which grants them a genuine life and orients their existence, is the participation within these truths…presupposes the construction…of an apparatus by means of which truths can be discerned: an apparatus by means of which one can circulate among truths and render them compossible. And all this in terms of contemporaneity…it starts from life and ends at life.[167]

For Badiou, within ecology "is the struggle to continue the pure existence of the collective,"[168] arguing for a move beyond the limits of *democratic materialism* if philosophy is to have meaning again and if there is to be any value in *thinking* political change. Such a position entails a new positioning for ethics as well, if it is to escape the trap of mere opinion as the "anarchic debris of circulating knowledge."[169] Such an ethical form acts as simulacra, and to counter this, Badiou calls for an ethics that combines discernment, courage, and moderation.[170] In place of a regulating moral order, ethics should be redefined as a construction of truths that are localizable, specific and singular. Thus, if "ethics" invokes a contemporary nihilism, a retreat from ethics and a movement instead toward *situations* and *singular processes* becomes necessary.[171] In his essay "One Divides into Two," Badiou uses Nietzsche to critique a moral argument about the "grosse Politik" of Mao and Lenin, arguing that moralizing about politics is a residue of the old world. The projects of Lenin and Mao reflected the failure of the historical idea of the vanguard party and its attendant *passion for the real*, which is itself the premise behind Badiou's articulation of a "politics without party." At the same time, however, Badiou does defend Lenin's theoretical foundation for philosophy:

> Our duty, supporting ourselves on Lenin's work, is to reactivate in politics, against the morose obsession of our times, the very question of thought...To all those who claim to practice political philosophy, we ask: What is your critique of the existing world? What can you offer us that's new? Of what are you the creator?[172]

Badiou's philosophy of the generic singularity links the philosophy of the event to the Platonic sign of the same. Peter Hallward argues that such an orientation "enables Badiou to salvage reason from positivism."[173] To adequately think through ecology today, this orientation must further involve an aggressive critique of *democratic materialism* through affirmative construction.

Badiou Against Heidegger

Badiou and Heidegger would agree that *being* is not something we can fully know. Yet the void in Heideggerian philosophy and the *revealing* that it entails through its *coming-to-be* leads merely, for Badiou, to a philosophy of contemplation. Badiou views Heidegger's process as a form of constructed nostalgia that can be seen as a kind of *speculative totalitarianism*. Badiou separates his approach from the Heideggerian *revealing* as a kind of conscious subtraction and deduction of the subject. If God is indeed dead, then philosophy is the articulation of *thought immanent to the multiple*. The foundation point must be the void. In *Being and Event*, Badiou argues that, "all thought supposes a situation of the thinkable, that is to say, a structure, a counting for one, whereby the presented multiple is consistent, numerable."[174]

Badiou proposes the de-statification of thought, or the subtraction of the subject from the state, writing "the central idea of my ontology is the idea that what the state seeks to foreclose through the power of its count is the void of the situation, and the event that in each case reveals it."[175] Badiou writes that, "the true essence of the wager is that we must wager."[176] The truth is a labour that must be constructed from the void, but is not the void made present. Badiou's philosophical project is a void-based ontology in which "the universal is only that which is an immanent exception."[177]

Badiou writes that, "truths are eternal because they are resubjec-tivizable, re-experimentable,"[178] however it is also true that truths exist outside of philosophy; they require identification and affirmation *as* truth. For Badiou, "philosophy is essentially axiomatic, and not definitional or descriptive."[179] Contra Heideggers's notion of revealing, Badiou advo-cates for a series of uncompleted movements that are in the direction of "withdrawal to intervention, from subtraction to transformation, from prescription to production."[180] For Heidegger, the event takes on a form of historicism, a being in time, whereas for Badiou, "what is past is void, irredeemably finished forever."[181] Even for an intricate problem like glob-al warming, however, nothing is too complex to be understood— nothing is inaccessible. For Badiou, since Nature is "composed entirely of natural elements," "all (that is natural) is (belongs) in all, except that there is not all." In other words, *Nature does not exist*, instead, science must expose what it, science, *is not*, or cannot reveal.[182]

The Truth

Truth, for Badiou, stands in a polar relationship to the Aristotelian view that truth inheres to the correct relation between language and things; claiming, rather, that real philosophy is a critique of this definition of truth. Truth should not be limited to a form of judgment, he argues, but should be a new creation, an act, and a process. Badiou contends that if all truth is first something new, the truth must be submitted to thought as a process in the real rather than as a judgment. Truth is first a relationship to happening while knowledge only creates a repetition, arguing that truth appears in its newness interrupting repetition, resulting in a rupture in the laws of the world not reducible to the common knowledge. The event belongs to the situation, beginning with both a negation and an affirmation. It is a negation because it is *undecidable, and* it is affirmative in the decision to name the event itself. To say that the event has taken place is to establish a trace of the event. Though the event is not calculable or demonstrable, one can decide to be faithful to its consequences. All new truths, as a consequence of the event, are the proposition of a new logic, a proposition for a new logic of existence itself.

The *organization of the consequences of an event,* are part of a finite verification towards an infinite truth. A truth, as such, is universal, as part of a generic subset that is not reducible to established knowledge. Badiou, states that a truth is inside the world, and goes beyond the limit point of the world, but it cannot be totalized within the world itself. At a given point in time, we wager that the event has taken place and must be adjudicated outside the established rules of knowledge. The construction of a truth is the process by which we measure what our times are capable of, though we remain within its impossibility. The engagement to the truth is the opening up of the field of possibility in the real, in a process by which, through creative action, something that is impossible becomes possible.[183]

Secondly, the new truth affirms a new boundary between the impossible and the possible. Philosophy attempts to recuperate and make visible the contradiction between the state of affairs and being, thereby displacing the boundary and carving a path for a new freedom. Badiou argues that it is better to have a disaster than a lack of being. When we are seized by an event it changes something of the real in our subjective situation, ultimately operating as a rupture of the active determination of life.

The question of the destruction of Nature is a political question, but also a broader philosophical question, about the global organization of human collectivity. Ecology actively critiques the idea that the capitalist market is more important than the natural world, proposing that human life is disconnected from Nature. An event related to this problem of the relation between human life and Nature will make a distinction between the life of the people and the organization of the life of the people by capital and the state, requiring a manner of thinking beyond the binary of the desperate poor and the nihilistic rich, according to Badiou. There is the collective desire for a new world and the desire for the true life, where freedom is crucial to the true life. Truth is made up of bodies and languages—concrete processes in the world; it is a *production* in the world. It is in this way that a relationship between truth and political action in the world is understood, compounded by the emergence of a new subject inside this participation to the becoming of a new truth.

The alternative to any paralyzing nihilism of the present will be the materiality of novelty and the invention of truths.[184] Badiou observes:

> Every age—and in the end, none is worth more than any other—has its own figure of nihilism. The names change, but always under these names ('ethics' for example) we find the articulation of conservative propaganda with an obscure desire for catastrophe.[185]

Within this dialectic is not the relation between one form of power against an equal power. The relation, rather, is between one side that is powerful and another side that is not. Badiou's ontology puts forward two specific propositions: Firstly, that mathematics is ontology, and secondly, that "the new happens in being under the name of the event."[186] With these propositions, Badiou proposes a *materialist dialectics* and the development of a new praxis. In Badiou's ontology, philosophy must think through the compossibility of truth procedures in the four domains of science, love, politics, and art. For Badiou, truths occur outside and independently of philosophy. The philosopher arrives much later, but must *attempt* to arrive early enough. The question of ecology, as such, falls within the problem of thinking the relation between *change* and *being*—properly, falling inside the ques-

tion of the subject. Badiou calls for a mobile philosophy that is neither
a place of sovereignty nor fused to its truth procedures, "embrac[ing] a
certain anxiety, obsession and desire: the mix which fuels its circulation between the history of philosophy, a theory of the subject, truth
and appearing, and contemporary truth procedures."[187] Ultimately,
change in the world under the sign of equality, for Badiou, involves
understanding the question: *What is the genericity of truths that are
being produced as a consequence of the event?*

A critique of Badiou's work centres on the lack of a formal
distinction between "the subjectivization in a truth procedure and
ideological interpellation."[188] For Badiou, the subject *writes the event
into being,* through an act of fidelity,[189] distinguishing the *subtractive*
movement from the Heideggerean notion of the withdrawal of being.
It is not in this withdrawal that being allows for forgetting in order
to assign a poetic overturning, rather, "it is in being foreclosed from
the presentation that being as such is constrained to be sayable, for
humanity, within the imperative effect of a law, the most rigid of all
conceivable laws, the law of demonstrative and formalizable infer-
ence."[190] In this sense, Badiou's ontology can be grasped as a theory
of the void. The state always re-presents what is already presented as a
representative of the ruling class.[191] The "mark" is the excrescence of
the state and can be seen in its *re-presentation* rather than its presentation. It is indicative of the excess of the state. Politics stakes its
existence in drawing a relation between void and excess, according to
Badiou. He writes:

> Rather than a warrior beneath the walls of the State, a political activist
> is a patient watchman of the void instructed by the event, for it is only
> when grappling with the event that the State blinds itself to its own
> mastery. There the activist constructs the means to sound, if only for
> an instant, the site of the unpresentable, and the means to be thence-
> forth faithful to the proper name that, afterwards, he or she will have
> been able to give to—or hear, one cannot decide—this non-place of
> place, the void.[192]

This forceful capture of the empty place is a means of seizing truths in philosophy at the scale of the infinite insofar as it is an attempt at articulating a universal truth. As Badiou elaborates, "in its most abstract form, the recognition of the infinity of being is first of all the recognition of the infinity of situations, the supposition that the count-as-one concerns infinite multiplicities." [193] In contrast to a thinker like Hegel who renounced the possibility of ontology being a situation, Badiou proposes to break the ontological immanence of the one. Infinity splits, instead, into bad and good.

Against Human Rights

Human rights can be critiqued as a normative Western framework that masks ideological constructions of geopolitical power. Badiou (through Lyotard) does, however, make a case for human rights being defined as the rights of the infinite, rather than as laws put forward and arbitrated by the UN or courts of law. Furthermore, he states that we can recover democracy as a term provided that the definition is subtracted from its limited state form. In concordance with Badiou, Žižek has also makes forceful arguments against human rights, in his essay, *Against Human Rights,* he writes:

> Contemporary appeals to human rights within our liberal-capitalist societies generally rest upon three assumptions. First, that such appeals function in opposition to modes of fundamentalism that would naturalize or essentialize contingent, historically conditioned traits. Second, that the two most basic rights are freedom of choice, and the right to dedicate one's life to the pursuit of pleasure (rather than sacrifice it for some higher ideological cause). And third, that an appeal to human rights may form the basis for a defense against the 'excess of power'.[194]

Žižek argues that political space is never pure and that it relies on pre-political violence, such as the original formation of the legal order itself, where the origin myth of the law itself is covered over by violent lies. Therefore, he argues that, "the task of critical analysis is to discern the hidden political process that sustains all these 'non' or 'pre'-political

relationships. In human society, the political is the encompassing structuring principle, so that every neutralization of some partial content as
'non-political' is a political gesture *par excellence*."[195] The universality of
human rights, then, must be deconstructed from its ideological conception. As Žižek continues:

> 'Man', the bearer of human rights, is generated by a set of political
> practices which materialize citizenship; 'human rights' are, as such, a
> false ideological universality, which masks and legitimizes a concrete
> politics of Western imperialism, military interventions and neo-colo-
> nialism… How—in what specific historical conditions—does abstract
> universality become a 'fact of (social) life'? In what conditions do
> individuals experience themselves as subjects of universal human
> rights?[196]

For Badiou, a conception of ethics built around human rights is
problematic by its very premise:

> Every intervention in the name of civilization *requires* an initial con-
> tempt for the situation as a whole, including its victims. And this is why
> the reign of 'ethics' coincides, after decades of courageous critiques of
> colonialism and imperialism, with today's sordid self-satisfaction in the
> 'West', with the insistent argument according to the misery of the Third
> World is the result of its own incompetence, its own inanity—in short,
> of its *subhumanity*.[197]

In the materialist dialectics of Badiou, actual human rights are
defined as an affirmation of the body and language of the subject to
create truths outside the language and logic of the state. Badiou writes,
"a point is a moment in a truth procedure (such as a sequence of emancipatory politics) when a binary choice (do this *or* that) decides the future
of the entire process…any failure can be located *in a point*." [198] Thus
by determining *a priori* the framework of the ethical, the regime that it
establishes does not allow for thinking through the singularity of specific
situations. I would argue that Badiou's critical view of ethics is akin to
characteristics of the Greek term, *eu-oudénose*—"a smug nihilism."[199]
American writer Rebecca Solnitt argues that we need to begin a new
political sequence by overthrowing language, "because the revolt against

brutality begins with a revolt against the language that hides that brutality."[200] Ethics, as such a language, creates a normative moral order that is an ideological construction rather than something bearing any relation to true material meaning in the world. As Michael Taussig observes, "all societies live by fictions taken as real."[201] The world consists of situations with concrete exceptions, where each of these worlds exist in their true meaning from time to time. It is the work of philosophy to think through these subtractive exceptions and inscribe them into legibility concerning the question of ecology today.

The Evental Rupture and its Consequences

Badiou argues that there is a relation between the *event* and the *creation of a new possibility*. There is the production of something like a rupture in the active determination of life. If the generic is something universal, it is the task of philosophy to explain this miracle, according to Badiou. Deconstructing the question of ecology, we can claim that it is primarily shaped by the idea that the market is more important than Nature today. If we are to invent a new relation to Nature we must also invent something new in the collective organization of humanity under the name of the Idea, where the event will account for the opposition between the true life of the people and the organization of the life of the people under the state and capitalism. Truth is an active process and not a static ethical condition functioning as a law of the world. For Badiou, the truth, recovered from religion, is an expression of the Absolute, of the infinite, and is a magnificent and divine pleasure. The truth is part of a collective desire for a new world.

For Badiou, there is a relation between the creative desire of humanity and the oppressive aspect of humanity under the law of the market and state. For Badiou, every subject has the right to be free because equality calls for freedom for everybody. The truth under the sign of the event leaves the trace of affirmative ruptures, made up of bodies and languages and is part of the concrete processes in the world. In the articulation of political action and truth, the subject is an active participant in the becoming of a new truth. Freedom and truth are bedfellows, in the work of Badiou; they account for the creation of something new in light of something that happens. Truth is a production in the world that also distinguishes the difference between an individual and a subject, for it is inside the process of a truth where the formation of a new subject is thrust into a process of becoming. It is this materiality of novelty of the creation of something new that overcomes the paralyzing nihilism of each epoch. But, we should caution, the truth is not all. In every concrete world there is a limit point to the constructive *potency* of a truth.[202]

Philosophy's task is to prepare for the event by encouraging the movement of the impossible into the realm of the possible. Badiou states that first we must affirm that something impossible may in fact be possible through creative activity, highlighting the contradiction between the state of affairs and being. The event is the place and time where the ordinary rules of commonplace life do not apply - it is when the subject is seized by an event and something of the real in their subjective determination changes. In the Lacanian sense, the real is excessive and unbearable, but crucial to subjectivity, whereas for Badiou, the opening up to the real as part of becoming should be a joyous rupture, for it is an affirmation that the impossible exists.[203] What is called for today, inside the question of ecology, is a rupture between capitalism and modernity, in opposition to the abolition of future being proposed. It is my argument, that a *non-capitalist modernity* is a world that ecology proposes today. From the specifics of its localization, ecology proposes a universality in which everyone can participate in the name of equality. The political invention of truth will be an affirmative act of division, constructed at a distance from the state and capital, rather than an act of consensus. The event will constitute a seizure of truths. As Badiou writes, "we are open to the infinity of worlds. To live is possible. Therefore, to (re)commence to live is the only thing that matters."[204]

Ecological Metapolitics proposes that, in their contemporary usage, the terms *political philosophy*, *environmental ethics, democracy*, and *human rights* are not relevant to the question of ecology insofar as they have become the captured language of *inoperativity* valorized by the limits imposed by *democratic materialism*. It is not an argument that we should give up on these words or on *this* or *that* language, but rather an argument for returning them to their proper meaning outside the state, and thereby opening up in them, the possibility of new political invention through the immanent rupture of creative novelty. Within the problem of ecology, this is an attempt to create *an outside*. Embedded in this idea, is that through the inertia of the event and the resulting fidelity of a newly created subject, the movement from the impossible to the possible can be constructed regarding the question of ecology today.

3

THE DIALECTIC OF RESISTANCE

War All The Time

In order to consider the paradox of ecology today, it is obviously necessary to consider fundamental changes to collective human living and to the very idea of what constitutes resistance — of the human desire to overcome the repetition of the world *as it is*, and to change the movement from the present to the future and the creative possibility of an outside. This movement from the present to the future is also the construction of a new history. If the question of ecology today is concerned with the proper organization of human life as a part of Nature, it is also concerned with how this relation is presently organized and with how to bring about a rupture with *what is*. Central to this notion is an understanding of resistance within the philosophical field as it portends the formation of the event. In his lectures collected in *Society Must Be Defended*, Michel Foucault asks a series of provocative questions, by inverting Carl von Clausewitz' observation, and instead asking 'is politics war by other means?':

> Can war serve as an analyzer of power relations?
>
> Must war be regarded as a primal and basic state of affairs, and must all phenomenon of social domination, differentiation, and hierarchicalization be regarded as its derivatives?
>
> Do processes of antagonism, confrontations, and struggles among individuals, groups or classes derive in the last instance from general practices of war?

Can a set of notions derived from strategy and tactics constitute a valid and adequate instrument for the analysis of power relations?...

How, when, and in what way did people begin to imagine that it is war that functions in power relations, than an uninterrupted conflict undermines peace, and that the civil order is basically an order of battle?[205]

Responding to the philosophical space opened up by Hobbes, Machiavelli, Clausewitz, and Nietzsche much earlier in their respective considerations of human nature and the organization of society, Foucault's lectures develop a genealogy of biopolitics that reflect the dialectical-material tension between the state and the subject through various techniques of governmentality. Foucault argues that confrontations and struggles in the capital-parliamentary framework move situations from a state of actual war into a domesticated symbolic order of legitimated combat sanctioned by the state on the side of powerful interests, in a process Badiou refers to, disparagingly, as the "pantomime" of state politics. With Foucault, there is not a static victim. As he famously writes in *The History of Sexuality*, "where there is power, there is resistance." [206]And, as he once articulated in an interview:

... if there was no resistance there would be no relations of power. Because everything would be simply a question of obedience. From the moment an individual is in the situation of not doing what they want, they must use relations of power. Resistance thus comes first, it remains above all the forces of the process, under its effect it obliges relations of power to change. I thus consider the term "resistance" to be the most important word, the key word of this dynamic.[207]

Clausewitz also presented the argument that modern politics and war both *pivot* on the *capacity to resist*. Troublingly, Foucault argues that resistance precedes power. Foucault does not ascribe to Hannah Arendt's idea of *total domination*, but allows for the possibility (similarly to Hegel) that the oppressed have sites and modes of resistance. According to philosopher Howard Caygill, Arendt underestimates the *capacity to resist* in her elaboration of the condition of total domination, since she believes that under total domination, it is possible to turn the human being in to a *mere thing.*[208] But with discrete acts of resistance there exists a broader capacity to resist. It is a matter of sequences and consequences in the construction of the present. There is a need for an affirmative understanding of resistance framed in terms of interruption, invention, creative novelty, and judgment as these fit inside the question of the subject. In asserting the affirmation of resistance, Badiou distinguishes his definition of politics from Arendt as follows:

> For Arendt, politics concerns "living together," the regulation of being together as a republic, or as public space. It's not an adequate definition. It reduces politics to the sole instance of judgment, and eventually to opinion, rather than recognizing that the essence of politics concerns thought and action, as connected through the practical consequences of a prescription.[209]

If we are to assume that war is a primal and basic state of affairs, as Foucault suggests in *Society Must Be Defended*, how is political change to be constructed and mobilized by a subject as a consequence of the event? How then can we apply this idea of war to analyze power relations and resistance within the question of ecology today? [210]

Additionally, for Serres, "Dialectics can be reduced to the eternal return, and the eternal return of wars brings us to the world." [211] He argues, even further that:

> History begins with war, understood as the closure and stabilization of violent engagement within juridical decisions. The social contract that gave birth to us is perhaps born with war, which presupposes a prior agreement that merges with the social contract...War is the motor of history: history begins with war and war set history on its course. But since, in the straitjacket of the law, war follows the repetitive dynamics of violence, the resulting movement, which follows the same laws, mimics an eternal return. [212]

This Hobbesian idea of war of all against all is a philosophical trope that has right and leftist variations, and problematizes liberal humanist modes of organizational and structural de-politicization.

Clausewitz

The work of Clausewitz is essential to understanding strategic and tactical theories of resistance. He should more accurately be read as a theoretician of resistance than as a theoretician of war, according to Caygill. For Clausewitz, *zweck* (purpose) is the aim of war, and with its appearance is always the capacity to resist. It is the fusion of politics and war that creates the absent other of resistance. There is a note of caution in Clausewitz that "war as a means of continuing or actualizing political logic threatens to take the place of politics that it should serve."[213] War and politics are not the same—they are proximal with one another, "it has its own grammar, but not its own logic."[214] Resistance, then, distorts the grammar of war by displacing the single act with duration of struggle or a protracted war of resistance. It is a fight *in* and *for* time. The ecological question today, particularly the consequences of global warming that extend beyond human life cycles, suspends, draws out, and interrupts even further the temporal and spatial considerations of resistance. As Clausewitz asks, "what influence can this resistance have, what are its conditions and how is it to be applied?"[215]

Caygill's reading of Clausewitz articulates resistance as, "a protracted attack on the enemies material and moral resources…goal of the pure war of resistance is the capacity to resist over time."[216] The strategic task is to erode the material resources and political will of the enemy. In Clausewitz, we find a distinction between *positive war* aimed at destroying the enemy and *negative war* aimed at destroying the enemy's logic of combat by exhausting or eroding its resources with the combination of resistance and duration. For Clausewitz, war is the breakdown of the alliance between reason and politics, and the uncertainty of sequences and chance that separates out planning from the actuality of conflict - what he terms *friction*.

Clausewitz also articulates the complexity and subtlety of a *People's War:*

> According to our representation of People's War, it must be a foggy
> or cloudlike being that will never allow itself to be concentrated into a
> resistant body, otherwise the enemy will apply an appropriate force to
> this kernel, destroy it and take a number of prisoners: thus morale will
> sink, all will consider that the main question has been decided, further
> effort useless and the weapons fall out of the hands of the people.[217]

If attendant to the question of ecology is the question of the subject
of change, then *resistance of duration and scale* is relevant as an object
of thinking change. Within any strategy of war in politics, or of a strategy
of change more broadly, is the assumption of *friction*.

A Case for Permanent Resistance

Whether violent or non-violent, Caygill argues that,

> resistance is motivated above all by a desire for justice, its acts are
> performed by subjectivities possessed of extreme courage and fortitude
> and its practice guided by prudence, all three contributing to the delib-
> erate preservation and enhancement of the capacity to resist.[218]

Resistance is not simply a resistance against the dominant power;
according to Caygill, it is rooted in something like a universal justice. For
Clausewitz, war is both a *function* and a *failure* of the political world. For
Lenin, Mao, and Che, resistance can and does include violence as a legitimate means to an end. Gandhi and Gene Sharp, by contrast, argue for
preserving and enhancing the capacity to resist in the process of non-violent direct action. A protracted war of resistance, then, can be violent or
non-violent, or a mixture of the two, as is demonstrated by the distinct
20th-century examples of Mao, Mahatma Gandhi, and Nelson Mandela.[219]

There are perfectly moral reasons to simultaneously interrogate both
the coercive non-violence and monopoly on violence of the victorious
order that polices contemporary common ideology. In that sense, and according to Caygill, challenging the ethical primacy of a non-violent morality and subjectivity is a legitimate site of contestation. In his reading of

the *Communist Manifesto*, Caygill identifies the importance of "translating resistance into the logic of a conscious political project oriented to the future,"[220] representing a link between the present resistance and a duty of care for the future of the movement. Revenge becomes a form of justice when there are not other means of adjudication. Nietzsche's notion of *ressentiment* comes with the desire for vengeance, linking it to both the Christian and socialist traditions. As Caygill elaborates,

> The socialist, the anarchist, the nihilist—in as much as they find in their existence something of which someone must be *guilty,* they are still the closest relations of the Christian, who also believes he can better endure his sense of sickness and ill-constitutedness by finding someone whom he can make responsible for it. The instinct of revenge and *ressentiment* appears here in both cases as a means of enduring, as instinct of self-preservation.[221]

For Caygill, there is a desire to move from *ressentiment* to an affirmative, inventive resistance; exiting a logic of *ressentiment* in order to escape oppositional logics. The desire for justice carried out in resistance is built around the ability to sustain courage over time; it is by its premise, conditioned on a spatial and temporal logic. Resistance defined as a form of fidelity to the event leaves traces and forms part of the archive of political struggle, where the subject forms an affirmative, resistant subjectivity as a consequence of the event. It is in this fashion where we can map a relation between Caygill's idea of affirmative inventive resistance and Badiou's notion of affirmative dialectics.

Time/Space Resistance

Political change, especially regarding the question of ecology, is certainly not a linear project. Rather, Caygill's notion of the capacity to resist involves interruption, a flickering out, a beginning again, a stumbling forth, a circling back. With every advance comes any number of false promises, betrayals, and confused fidelities. Neither is political change a transparent process, nor is there a familiar cadence to its grammar and working logic. It begins with a wager in time and space.

Just as the words "political philosophy," "environmental ethics," "democracy," and "human rights" have lost much of their public meaning, Caygill argues that "non-violent resistance was in danger of becoming a moralism that superficially negates the symptoms of violence without recognizing how its non-violence remains implicated in violence and war."[222] For him, non-violence has to be proven against the claims of war. Badiou argues that the subject to an event must function at the scale of the adversary. Gandhi's strategy of *satyagraha* (insistence on truth) is one example that functioned on a large scale over a long period in a colonial context. The Zapatistas' movement, calling for "*everything for everyone, nothing for us*," is another example of the establishment of a political logic constructed from outside the state into an affirmative inventive resistance that moves from the singular to the universal.

With political action seen as a war of movement, Antonio Gramsci identifies the crucial importance of creative action in resistance. Gramsci also considers it important to determine if the state is a thing or a process, arguing that unity is needed for a bundle of forces to create change, functioning at multiple velocities and differing degrees of intensity. It is a resistance of the *long durée* possessing features that are simultaneously public and clandestine to move in the direction that advances the position of a movement over time.[223]

Walter Benjamin emphasizes interruption and the potential vested in the future (past), whose *jetztzeit* (time of the now) is made available for the future. Benjamin argues that the present generation, by looking both backward and forward, are as much the future for the past, and are the past for the future. Benjamin calls this a weak messianic power, a power on which the past has a claim; for him we are already living in a state of war where the theatre of battle spans the past, present, and future, arguing that the state of exception is the rule. He locates resistance in a politics of speed and time, writing that we are the messianic generation of the past. The capacity to resist is distinct from the revolutionary project of realizing full freedom. Benjamin's articulation in *Theses on History* of this relationship of past, present, and future bears a direct relation to the question of ecology today, for inscribed in Benjamin's work is a critique of the modernist project and its attendant ideology of linear progress.[224]

The Situationists

The relation between the death drive and the pleasure principle of *jouissance* is essential to understanding the role of resistance. The violence of a world to be created may supplant the violence of a world that destroys itself. The ecological project is in keeping with the Zapatistas' call to stand for the living, the dead, and those-yet-to-come. In their call for "everything for everyone and nothing for us," is a recognition that the resistant subject is already dead, and as Caygill writes, "the resistant subject is not free to choose a life of resistance, but is already dead so *must* resist."[225]

Guy Debord articulated the problem of the limits of capitalism, spectacle, and the planet in his 1971 essay "The Sick Planet." He writes:

> It reveals itself everywhere as ideology and it gains on the ground as real process. These two [mutually] antagonistic movements—the supreme stage of commodity production and the project of its total negation, equally rich in internal contradictions—grow together. They are the two sides through which a single historical moment (long-awaited and often foreseen in inadequate partial figures) manifests itself: the impossibility of the continuation of the functioning of capitalism. [226]

Debord defines "revolt as a *materialist* demand of the exploited."[227] What is radically different about the question of ecology today is that *it no longer has any time* and now awaits its perfect material conclusion.[228] The conflict of "modern productive forces" has entered its last phase, proceeding past accumulation to the eventual production of death. Debord argues that, "the problem of the degradation of the totality of the natural and human environment…radically becomes the problem of the *material possibility for existence* of a world that pursues such a movement."[229] The politics of this time, according to Debord, require historical consciousness as the inevitable conclusion to continue the world as it is, as it approaches the reality of its finitude. Debord writes,

> The conflict of modern productive forces and the bourgeois or bureaucratic relations of production of capitalist society has entered nto its final phase. The production of non-life has more and more pursued its linear and cumulative process; over-coming a final threshold in its progress, it now directly produces death.[230]

The enemy is no longer an illusion but *is* death. Debord argues that since state systems are essentially conservative insofar as they maintain a capitalist order, it is necessary to take hold of a power that works against the current hegemony. Debord describes what Badiou would define as a *point*. Debord argues that there is a choice "between a thousand fortunate or disastrous possibilities that are relatively correctable and, on the other hand, annihilation."[231] The dialectical relation between courage and anxiety, that Badiou identifies as built into the question of resistance today, can also lead to *seinsvergessenheit*—a forgetfulness of being. As we become the authors of our own collective disasters and catastrophes, these torsions that define our existence lead to a crisis of being and, more generally, a crisis of the collective.

Raoul Vaneigem, another writer associated with the Situationists, writes that, "in the scope of power there is no future other than a past reiterated…Power's crowning achievement, in its attempt to trap people into identifying with such a past future, lies in its resort to historical ideology."[232] A duty of care for the future must undergird the question of ecology today. How is it possible to build an orientation of collective human existence that creates a repetition on the side of Nature and all living beings, as part of a new modern tradition that does not reproduce the disasters of the last century? There is a stench in the air today of what Benjamin called *left melancholy*—of a movement not up to the challenge posed by the scale of capital. The progressive left is the proverbial *fist in papier-maché*. It portends the nihilistic culture of the oppositional logic, of moral victories alone, and of innumerable defeats—a movement inadequate for the time, living-in-formaldehyde, beset by exhaustion.

State of Exception

Foucault describes an apparatus as having a dominant strategic function in three ways. First, an apparatus is an element of history composed of sets of institutions, processes of subjectivization, and forces of coercion through power relations that become solidified. Secondly, an apparatus is a set of practices and procedures that attempt to instrumentalize their ends to obtain an effect that is immediate. Thirdly, apparatuses materially produce their subjects. For Agamben, an apparatus is "anything that has in some way the capacity to capture, orient, determine, intercept, model, control, or secure the gestures, behaviors, opinions, or discourses of living beings. A Subject is that which results from the fight between living beings and apparatuses." [233]

The expansion of apparatuses through historical, cultural, and technological means, corresponds to the proliferation of processes of subjectification for Agamben. Personal identity and individual freedom of a subject in this governmentalized and ordered world becomes a masquerade. The logic to resist is what Agamben calls the "everyday hand to hand struggle with apparatuses." [234] The capture, subjectification, and domestication of the human desire for happiness involves the terrain of struggle between the repetition of the capitalist subjectivity and political change regarding the ecological question today. Agamben writes, "the capture and subjectification of this desire in a separate sphere constitutes the specific power of the apparatus." [235]

Following Foucault's position, Agamben proclaims that, "without the process of subjectification within the apparatus, it would just be violence."[236] The apparatus aims to create inoperative but free bodies through this process of desubjectivization. Agamben argues that the very technologies that give us our freedom like the cell phone and the internet, are the very mechanisms of control that place us in the double bind. For Agamben, the machine is aimlessly leading us to catastrophe; we are captured by various degrees of intensity but are not under total domination. In this catch-22, is what Agamben calls the *eclipse of politics*. It is the death of a politics that presupposes the existence of subjects, and is thereby seen as a process of desubjectivation and inoperativity – a direct undermining of political potency. Agamben argues that we are already in a state of exception and of global civil war today; in a sense, we are all *homo sacer*. Foucault, by comparison, writes, "we are animals in whose politics our very life as living beings is at stake."[237] Here we might also consider the distinction between *zoe* and *bios,* as elaborated by Arendt's *Human Condition* to be the basis for Agamben's definition of biopolitics.

In Agamben's vision, it is the task of politics to intervene in our processes of desubjectivation and reveal "the Ungovernable who are the beginning and vanishing point of politics" if we are to overcome, what he calls, the "era of the lost gesture."[238] Agamben observes that modern man has been deprived of his biography, contending that in today's *state of exception*—now very much the rule—"nothing looks more like a terrorist than the ordinary man."[239] The state of exception is the point of imbalance between public law and political fact at the intersection of the legal and the political, as well as between juridical order and life.[240] Though it has a relationship to civil war, revolution, and insurrection, the state of exception is primarily applied as the state's response to domestic conflict, in what Agamben calls *the voluntary creation of a permanent state of emergency*. What we can observe today, however, is a transition from an "exception" to a *de facto* technique of government. With the suspension of the juridical order, the legal status of the individual becomes extinguished indefinitely. For Agamben, thinking is what makes life possible –

it must be able to give back possibility, or potentiality. Inside of memory, what was achieved becomes again possible. Potentiality is inscribed in the transmission of possibility.

Agamben has diagnosed contemporary governments as having more power than ever before, to the diminishment of the citizenry's rights. Endemic to the state of exception is the state's subjective right to its self-preservation, wherein the state ultimately subtracts itself from the consideration of the law, ultimately suspending the law, rather than enacting new ones. The power to suspend and to decide on the nature of the exception remains the sovereign right of the state, where pure violence is included in the law through its very exclusion. The violence of the law is not outside the law – the state maintains a monopoly on the use of force. The production of the legal subject exists within the law. In its movement of construction and legitimation, the law amplifies its own power. It preserves the violence of the state. There is no law without violence. It acts as a means for regulating and adjudicating conflicting human interests. There is violence in *law-making* and *law-preserving*. There is in the origin myth of the law, the denial of the establishment of the apparatus after the injury, *ex post facto*. The relation between the market and the state becomes a constellation of power that has a bearing on the law. Politics suffers since it comes to be contaminated by the law. Agamben argues that political action is that which breaks the nexus between violence and the law. He references Carl Schmitt in articulating, within the birth of the camp, the difference between localization, *Ortung,* and order, *Ordnung.*[241] The "camp" today includes immigrants, refugees, and the colonized. For Christian Parenti, a theorist of climate change and geopolitics, "immigrants are the canaries in the political coal mine, and immigration is the vehicle by which the logic of the 'state of emergency' is smuggled into everyday life, law, and politics."[242] For Agamben, the working class movement shares with capitalism a notion of productivity, for the working person is equally a site of production and is therefore part of complicity with capital. The human animal will act as a device or a tool to ascribe action and responsibilities, where willing is deployed as a motor of responsibility. What does it mean to constitute oneself as a subject? It is a reflection on what the true life is. How do living beings make use of concepts? How can a living being become familiar with its own body? What emerges is the idea, historically, for Agamben, that the being is not a substance, but only a usage.

The notion of a good life emerges as an action in the world, becoming a relationship with the tool and the use of the thing. In that movement, the relation to things becomes broken. As Agamben relates, in medieval times there was a great danger of the monk who would lose his faith and experience a deep melancholy where his inability to do anything resulted in a loss of an immediate relationship to life. This melancholic state of being denotes a representation of breaking the notion of usage. It denoted not the loss of God, but the loss of the way leading to God. For Agamben, there was a desire to fill the instinctual lack of man. There was a lack of our presence in ourselves – an excess that puts us in the peculiar situation of exile in the world. In the human, and in their collective organization, is a suspension of the animal relation. We are born without work, but work is a condition of our relation to an apparatus.

What distinguishes humans from plants and animals? In Agamben's reading of Christian liturgy, the soul of the living moves in and out of death. Within this movement is the counter-tendency for dispossession and injustices of state power. The law designates an attempt for justice, retribution and repair, presenting a speculative claim that seeks recourse to the distant past, structuring temporality and preserving itself through coercive means. The practice of the care of the self informs subjectivity, and is the primary means and process through which people subjectivize themselves. In this *handiness,* what results is a being who cares. In this sense, *existing,* in and of itself, becomes a form of justice.

The devices of emancipation reveal our movements, relationships, and sequences of action. Our very mode of being, and our capacity to move from the one to the collective, is in a state of permanent capture.

Looking beyond the law as the site of organization, Agamben recalls the time of before law, identifying the phenomenon of the *oath, commandment*, and *will*, looking beyond the finitude of the state and the enclosures it places on the political possibilities of the future. Agamben argues that power requires inoperativeness precisely because inoperativeness is *captured* by power. In Agamben's etymological research, we find new modes of resistance from ancient times. Our capacity to define and resist the apparatus is absolutely crucial to reframing the problem of ecology today.

State as Solution?

In the language of geopolitics and military planning, the problem of global warming is a *threat multiplier.* It has the power to exacerbate existing tensions that already function within and between states and it reframes a condition of fear into the political space with potentially infinite consequences. Military planners argue that, in response to the evidence of climate change, the state is in the process of moving from the modern era of relative stability to a state of permanent emergency. Military strategists, by extension, write documents speculating on the future of global conflicts that will be exacerbated by impacts of global warming. In thinking through the ecological question, however, they simply orient their arguments around the continued defense of national security. Through the language, the writing, the dissemination, and its reception, a new apparatus emerges to uphold a continued construction of a world premised on the logic of the state. Christian Parenti, for his part, contends that we have run out of time for a total solution in our waiting for the utopian revolution to come, claiming that either capitalism solves the crisis or it destroys civilization.[243] Parenti suggests (in a tone distinctly against the position of Badiou) for a larger role for the state in the political solution that is to be constructed—for an active return to its role as a redistributor of income, social programs, and the public good.

In the context of real emergencies and real weather disasters, Parenti contends, it is the state that must be called upon. He theorizes that even though neoliberalism has minimized the state as a serious object of study, global warming will force a return of the state, urging us to negotiate any emancipatory political project with a re-engagement with the possibilities of statehood. While on the one hand, Parenti acknowledges that the crisis-driven return of the state also heralds a possible return to new apparatuses of repressive and undemocratic features such as the expansion of police powers and heightened biometric surveillance, he wagers, on the other hand, that it could also lead to a democratic renovation of government's progressive functions such as industrial regulation and wealth redistribution:

> Because of its magnitude the climate crisis can appear as if it is the combination of all environmental crises—overexploitation of the seas, deforestation, overexploitation of freshwater, soil erosion, species and habitat loss, chemical contamination, and genetic contamination due to transgenic bioengineering. But halting greenhouse gas emissions is a much more specific problem; it is only one piece of the apocalyptic panorama. Though all these problems are connected, the most urgent and all encompassing of them is anthropogenic climate change…We cannot wait for a socialist, or communist, or anarchist, or deep ecology, neo-primitive revolution; nor for a nostalgia-based *localista* conversion back to the mythical small-town economy of preindustrial America as some advocate.[244]

One can define politics outside of the limitations of the state (as Badiou does), while still keeping the state in the field of play. To be a subject outside the state is not necessarily to evacuate the terrain of struggle that involves the possibility of state action as part of the solution. One can be on the outside pushing in, without being subsumed or corrupted by the inside. As Badiou articulates,

> What we would say now is that there are a certain number of questions regarding which we cannot posit the absolute exteriority of the state. It is rather a matter of requiring something from the state, of formulating with respect to the state a certain number of prescriptions or

statements…This is what we mean by *prescriptions against the state.* This is not to say that we participate in the state. We remain outside the electoral system, outside any party representation. But we include the state in our political field, to the extent that, on a number of essential points, we have to work more through prescriptions against the state than in any radical exteriority to the state. [245]

The subtraction from the state that Badiou advocates does not evoke a pure non-relation to the state; it is a subtraction allowing the invention of a new political subject and a new definition of the truth outside the state. Ultimately the state can remain in the field of play of political possibility, even when we initiate "prescriptions" against it.

Coulthard: Fanon's Reading of Hegel

In the context of Indigenous struggles and decolonization, recognition through the state is increasingly critiqued as simply a reinscription of the logic of the state onto a localized situation. Dene Nation theorist Glen Coulthard, for example, suggests that there is a need to "challenge the now hegemonic assumption that the structure of domination that frames Indigenous-state relations can actually be undermined via a liberal politics of recognition."[246] Recognition through state mediation reproduces asymmetrical and non-reciprocal relations, he argues, in an observation sharing common ground with Badiou's critique of the state and the need for substraction in order to establish a new political sequence.

What Fanon, Badiou, and Coulthard share is a critique of classical Hegelian dialectics. For Hegel, "'self-consciousness exists in and for itself when, and by the fact that, it so exists for another; that is, it exists only in being acknowledged'."[247] Hegel moves beyond the relational nature of subjectivity, as Coulthard articulates, to "intersubjective conditions needed for the *realization of human freedom.*"[248] Fanon likewise argues that *being-for-itself* is compromised by the dependent consciousness of the slave, and it is Fanon's observation, as Coulthard identifies, where the need to move beyond patterns of domination and equality presents itself. It was Fanon's work as a psychotherapist that allowed him to observe how "subjectivities of the oppressed can be deformed by *mis-* or *non*-recognition."[249] Fanon asserts that colonial systems of governance rely as much on the *internalization* of racist recognition as they do on brute force. Through this process of internalization, a colonized population is easily transformed into subjects of imperial rule. Yet the derogatory framing of the slave by the master results in an unequal exchange in patterns of recognition. In his analysis of Fanon, Coulthard observes the necessity of the "subjective realm of colonialism [to] be the target of strategic transformation along with the socioeconomic structure."[250] Fanon thereby renovates Marxism, Coulthard concludes, by arguing beyond class relations that racism and its effects on the subject "are attributed a substantive capacity to structure the character of social relations."[251] When the upheaval of freedom comes from without, without struggle, that is, the dialectical progression of reciprocity is compromised. This type of "upheaval [does] not make a difference in the Negro," as Fanon states in *Black Skin, White Masks*, "[h]e [goes] from one way of life to another, but not from one life to another."[252]

It is Fanon's observation that it is only through struggle and conflict that imperial subjects overcome the arsenal of complexes and find their proper place. Without this struggle, this self-transformation cannot occur—foreclosing on the realization of authentic freedom. Similar to Ghandi's analysis, resistance that is not a foundational challenge will result in "white liberty and white justice." Without resistance of this kind, conflict, disruption, and the terms of recognition remain in the possession of the incumbents of power. The values of the colonial regime will "seep" into the colonized and limit the realm of possibility of their freedom by avoiding the adequate critique of inherent power structures. With this in mind, Fanon attests for "overcoming the processes of psycho-existential complexes through a process of strategic desubjectification."[253]

In a further critique of the master-slave dialectic, Fanon writes that, "for Hegel there is reciprocity" but in the colonies, "the master laughs at the consciousness of the slave. What he wants from the slave is not recognition but work." [254] Coulthard writes that with the "relations of domination between nation-states and sub-state national groups they 'incorporate' into their territorial and jurisdictional boundaries, there is no mutual dependency in terms of a need or desire for recognition."[255] In this way, the dialectic breaks down either by non-recognition of the equal status of the colonized population or by the strategic domestication of the terms of recognition in such a way that the foundation of the colonial relationship remains relatively undisturbed. Coulthard professes that the "colonial powers will only recognize the collective rights and identities of Indigenous peoples insofar as this recognition does not throw into question the background legal, political and economic framework of the colonial relationship itself."[256] There is an inherent limitation to the possibilities of recognition when placed against overtly structural expressions of domination, which include discursive worlds of recognition that can shape subjectivities and, asymmetrically mould relations of domination. In other words, recognition by the state of historically colonized peoples can be a form of subjection. This is relevant to the question of ecology today insofar as indigenous relations, decolonization struggles, and conflicts over land use in Western and non-Western countries are situated in direct confrontation with the state and corporate interests such as mining, oil extraction, and other carbon-emitting activities that work against the continuity of Nature as such. A distancing from the state and a *looking away* from the master, as Fanon describes it, is precisely the way many indigenous groups have been resisting these interests both historically and currently. They probably also provide one of the most effective ways to resist capitalist exploitation of Nature into the future as well.

From Fanon's perspective, there is little emancipatory potential in Hegel's politics of recognition but much in indigenous movements' own capacity to engage in collective self-affirmation. For Fanon, the colonized must struggle to reclaim their histories, traditions, and cultures; they must initiate processes of decolonization by recognizing themselves as free. This line of argumentation, against Hegel, is similar to Badiou's articulation of affirmative dialectics. For Fanon, it is necessary for a colonized people to *turn away* from the master and to struggle for freedom on its own terms and in accordance with its own values, moving beyond Hegel's simplistic binary put forward by the master-slave dialectic. In both Fanon and Badiou, there is a "calling forth" to truth by subjects of resistance: "At the very moment [the colonized come to] discover their humanity, they must begin to sharpen their knives to *secure its victory*."[257] Those struggling against colonialism and capitalism must *turn away*. Coulthard argues that Indigenous communities "have much to teach the Western world about the establishment of relationships within and between peoples and the natural world that are profoundly non-imperialist."[258] It should begin by not looking to that *other* for recognition.

Hegel's master-slave dialectic is what Fanon deems a *dual narcissism*. He critiques Hegel directly:

> For Hegel there is reciprocity; here the master scorns the consciousness of the slave...Likewise, the slave here can in no way be equated with the slave who loses himself in the object and finds the source of his liberation in his work. The black slave wants to be like his master. Therefore he is less independent than the Hegelian slave. For Hegel, the slave turns away from the master and turns toward the object. Here the slave turns toward the master and abandons the object.[259]

Fanon argues for a truth of the infinite: "In a fierce struggle I am willing to feel the shudder of death, the irreversible extinction, but also the possibility of impossibility."[260] He observes, moreover, that "self-division is a direct result of colonialist subjugation"[261] that leads to the "amputation of his being."[262] Existence still depends on a dialectical relation to the other—"man is only human to the extent to which he tries to impose his existence on another man in order to be recognized by him."[263] But in situations of colonial subjugation, a deferral to this dialectic is insufficient: "If you close the circuit...prevent the accomplishment of movement in two directions....deprives him of his *being-for-itself*."[264] It is a movement that concerns the "transformation of subjective certainty (*Gewissheit*) into objective truth (*Wahrheit*). Encountering resistance from the other leads to desire...a battle for the creation of a human world."[265]

Fanon provides important commentary on dialectics and colonialism that have much to offer regarding the question of ecology today. It is my position that Fanon and Badiou's work, though existing in different terminologies and ontologies, have a significant philosophical relationship to one another and offer emancipatory potential regarding the question of ecology we are currently facing.

Ecology today is concerned with the question of how to resist and how to invent a new, non-capitalist, modern tradition. In its reconfiguring of politics as thought, ecology must propose something like the idea of a new community coming forth. In theorizing "community as the inherent impossibility of our world," Badiou speaks to something "unavowable" (Maurice Blanchot), "inoperative" (Jean-Luc Nancy), or otherwise deferred: what Agamben would call a "coming community."[266] Badiou cites Book VI of the *Republic*, where Plato defines the sophist as one who cannot see "the extent to which the nature of the good and the nature of the necessary differ."[267] The problem of the world *as it is* can be articulated in this way for Badiou:

> the impossibility of the community, which is the real of the world, prevents politics from falling under an idea. It follows that every kind of politics essentially consists in managing necessity. Which can also be stated as: there is no emancipatory politics. What there is, is the regulated and natural development of liberal equilibria.[268]

In the separation of philosophy and politics, the need for de-suturing comes from this connection as a site of disaster for philosophy. Badiou proposes principles to delineate between these worlds and allow for philosophy to be a site of *compossibility*. The conditions of philosophy produce their own truths, where emancipatory politics exist as sequences under an eventual rupture.

4

ACCELERATIONIST GEOPOLITICS AND A NEW NOMOS OF THE ANTHROPOCENE

Toward a Nomos of the Anthropocene

Carl Schmitt, the controversial German legal and political theorist, addresses questions of sovereignty, land, the state, and international law in his work, *The Nomos of the Earth*. For Schmitt, the concept of *nomos*, from its Greek origins, had a meaning beyond the law, further signifying the "objectification of the *polis*,"[269] the development of which, Schmitt points out, was the most important part of *paideia* (education). For Plato, this notion of *paideia* transcended the importance of the written law,[270] wherein, the fixed aspects of Greek education were also named as *nomos*. As translator G.L. Ulmen writes, "For Schmitt, the nomos of the earth is the community of political entities united by common rules."[271] If sovereignty is concerned with power and the allocation of space regarding collective human living, the distribution of resources, and jurisdiction by states, then it is also a question concerning ecology.

For Plato, *nomos* signified *schedon*—a mere rule. Aristotle distinguished between the concrete order of the whole, *politeia*, and the individual *nomoi*. *Nomos* comes from the Greek—defined as "to divide" and "to pasture"—the measure by which land is divided and situated,[272] thus signifying enclosures in the spatial, literal sense. Schmitt defined the period from the Middle Age Christian demarcation of the European sphere (what he problematically refers to as the Age of Discovery to the end of the 19ᵗʰ century) as *jus publicum Europaeum,* an international order grounded in European public law. In this context *nomos* took on

85

the definition of norm, decision, and order, leading to Schmitt's foundational question, according to Ulmen as "'who decides?' with respect to questions such as: 'Which people are free? What is the content of true freedom?'" [273]

While technology renders some borders meaningless, states and state systems have increasingly become larger *Großräumen,* that is, larger political groupings that would arrange themselves into friends and enemies. With the introduction of the European idea of "just war," it brought into international law, the arbitrary, political, and self-serving nature of the Western orientation of customary international law. This international legal system, developed under European jurisprudence, relied on the legacy of Roman law and centuries of customs, according to Schmitt; serving as a *katechon*—a restrainer of total functioning law.[274] The change from the *republica Christiana* of the Middle Ages to a *jus public Europaeum* with the discovery of the New World and its colonization signified for Schmitt the first global order, based as it was on European sovereign states. Following that, the rise of U.S. power resulted in the end of European domination of the definition of customary international law by the end of the 19th century, punctuated by declarations such as the Monroe Doctrine that declared a *de facto* sphere of American influence over North and South America. The U.S. extended the three-mile limit of jurisdiction over the sea to over 300 miles, thereby "extending *Großraum* thinking over the free sea."[275] In Schmitt's work, however, there remains a Eurocentric spatial order based on his own politically biased observation that anti-colonial movements lack the capacity to create new spatial configurations.

In contrast to Schmitt's reductive polemics, contemporary indigenous writers such as Leanne Simpson, argue that an indigenous resistance needs to happen from within:

> We need to be able to articulate in a clear manner our visions for the future, for living as Indigenous Peoples in contemporary times. To do

so, we need to engage Indigenous processes, since according to our traditions, the processes of engagement highly influence the outcome of the engagement itself. We need to do this on our own terms, without the sanction, permission or engagement of the state, western theory or the opinions of Canada. [276]

Contrary to Schmitt, *Ecological Metapolitics* contends that anti-colonial movements not only have the capacity to orient and embed their own forms of spatial ordering outside of a Western framework, they are essential to the construction of a new modern tradition—a non-capitalist modernity. Considering that the capitalist framework is symptomatic of the problem of the Anthropocene, indigenous world-making and decolonization can be read as essential vectors in constructing an affirmative vision of the world from that which already is.

The European colonial project created a normative order of terrestrial existence involving both the division of space and the bracketing of war. As Schmitt quotes Goethe, writing in the time of Napoleon: "All pretty things have trickled away / Only sea and land count here."[277] There were three characteristics specific to this *nomos* of the earth that Schmitt identifies: First, he argues it provided an inner measure associated with the cultivation of the land; secondly, he proposes that cleared soil includes demarcations and divisions where lines are engraved and embedded; and thirdly, he posits that *nomos,* is delineated by fences, enclosures, boundaries, or structures.[278]

Schmitt proposes a view of an infinitely just earth—a *justissima tellus*[279]—in which the land is distinguished from the sea. The sea, in this vision, does not contain character, from the Greek *charassein*, defined as something in which to engrave, scratch, or imprint. The law of the sea differentiates the rights of states, but distinguishes these rights from those of mere pirates. As we can observe through Schmitt, this spatial ordering of free land and sea for 400 years was supported by a Eurocentric international law. We find further sympathy for it in a figure like Hegel, who asserted that, "the principle of family life is dependence on the soil, on firm land, on terra firma. Similarly, the natural element for industry, animating its outward movement, is the sea."[280]

The Christian Middle Ages in Europe were a pre-global spatial order that Schmitt argued was based on *imperium* (empire) and *sacerdotium* (priesthood), and on "a power that withholds" (*qui tenet*).[281] Crucially, Schmitt draws a distinction between *potestas* (power) and *auctoritas* (authority),[282] writing "in the connection between utopia and nihilism, it becomes apparent that only a conclusive and fundamental separation of order and orientation can be called 'nihilism' in an historical specific sense."[283] Schmitt, in his analysis, acknowledges that the movement of time inevitably creates a moment where a new order will be created:

> As long as world history remains open and fluid, as long as conditions are not fixed and ossified; in other words, as long as human beings and people have not only a past but also a future, a new nomos will arise in the perpetually new manifestations of world-historical events. Thus, for us, nomos is a matter of the fundamental process of apportioning space that is essential to every historical epoch—a matter of the structure-determining convergence of order and orientation in the cohabitation of peoples on this now scientifically surveyed planet…Every new age and every new epoch in the coexistence of peoples, empires, and countries, of rulers and power formations of every sort, is founded on new spatial divisions, new enclosures, and new spatial orders of the earth.[284]

For Schmitt, the new space of the new world did not create an enemy distinction but was viewed as free space – *terra nullius*.[285] The influences of the historical architecture of this period remain today. Schmitt identifies the Greenwich prime meridian, for example, as a relic of the British domination of the sea that was only accepted by French and German interests in the early 20th century.[286] There also remains today an attachment to a European, Christian calendar. During the period of European colonial expansion, he further observes, there was a distinction between the Spanish-Portuguese concept of *rayas* and the British/French concept of *amity lines*—both expressions of a spatial order that formed customary international law for the interests of the colonial powers.[287] *Rayas* and *amity lines* were therefore part of a European condition that assumed the *fait accompli* of Christianization.[288] In their introduction to customary international law, was the implicit assertion of the grounds for a just war, if peaceful attempts at free passage or free missions were denied.

This construction of legal concepts followed the philosophical space opened up by Francis Bacon and others. For them, the discovery of the new world and the natives originating there, stood outside humanity, as Schmitt relates via Hegel, the culture of the Mexicans and Peruvians "had to perish as soon as the (world-) spirit approached them."[289] These international laws thereby established the precedent of "discovery and occupation as legal title to land-appropriation."[290] *Jus publicum Europaeum* was driven by a *de facto* policy of state mercantilism, conforming to the Latin term *cujus regio, ejus economia*: "whose is the territory, his is the economy."[291] The colonizing power could take both public and private property by defining it as leaderless and its rule over indigenous peoples, coupled with theft of land, was delineated by a kind of *dominium eminens* (eminent domain).[292]

Ideas of sovereignty shifted with the discovery of the new world and its subsequent colonization and dispossession as Schmitt writes:

> Clearly, to the extent that overseas colonial territory became indistinguishable from state territory, in the sense of European soil, the structure of international law also changed, and when they became equivalent, traditional, specifically European international law came to an end.[293]

The problematic nature of this expansion of a specifically Eurocentric customary international law, and the political nature of its spatial ordering, was clearly impacted by its colonial expansion and by extension, its ideological foundations were called in to question by the changing orientation of global power:

> The belief in civilization and progress had become nothing more than an ideological façade...Essentially, the whole enterprise already was a helpless confusion of lines dividing spheres of interest and influence, as well as of failed amity lines simultaneously overarched and under-

mined by a Eurocentrically conceived, free, global economy ignoring all territorial borders. In this confusion, the old *nomos* of the earth determined by Europe dissolved. [294]

Schmitt identifies three specific features of power, arguing that, "the impulse to secrecy and to learn the secret is the first tendency of any power,"[295] referencing Hannah Arendt's observation that "real power begins where secrecy begins."[296] Secondly, he identifies "implicit centrality" as an apparatus that can "secure, justify and consolidate its position anew" regarding new corridors and access to power. Third is the countertendency of secrecy, he explains, which is the movement towards visibility and publicity.[297]

For Schmitt, appropriation and domination occurred in a complex set of customs, laws, and practices, writing that "the Eurocentric structure of nomos extended only partially as open land-appropriation and otherwise in the form of protectorates, leases, trade agreements and spheres of interest; in short, in more elastic forms of utilization."[298] Schmitt further identifies the third dimension of airspace as part of the new *nomos* under formulation in the 20th century.

Schmitt's analysis is intriguing and informative but totally problematic in terms of what he forecloses from the analysis, not to mention his real life political affiliations. He attempts to construct a theoretical topology of sovereignty over the earth by glossing over the obvious violence inherent to its historical process, keeping in line with his neo-authoritarian tendencies. Ultimately, Schmitt's argument is a conservative one that accounts for any conflict over power as part of a rational reordering and spatialization of land and the bracketing of war under the sign of the law. In making such sweeping claims in his theoretical work, Schmitt engages in a kind of epistemological violence, where, for him, the political is constituted in the state of exception and when complex political situations are reduced to a simplistic 'friend-enemy' distinctions. Despite the problematic nature of his political thought, his work is important to consider in thinking through the question of ecology today - particularly the challenges to the ideas of sovereignty that will emerge as a consequence of ecological crises and the challenges that information technology pose to historical and current traditions of state sovereignty. The Anthropocene, as an absolutely new historical event, will certainly create a new *nomos.* As Glen Coulthard points out in *Red Skin: White Masks: Rejecting the Colonial Politics of Recognition,* territorial dispossession is settler colonialism's specifically irreducible characteristic, where the state structures accumulation through dispossession. This process results in the transformation of non-capitalist forms of life into capitalist formulations. The connection to the land that is a part of human living for indigenous societies, is what Coulthard distinguishes as 'grounded normativity', in contrast to normative constructions of capitalist development. In the case of the Americas, of what Schmitt writes, is the European construction of the idea of *terra nullius,* the land belonging to no one. In such cases, sovereignty was constructed through settlement and the imposition of the legal order from without by colonial European powers – an historically verified genocidal project. For Coulthard, "primitive accumulation must be stripped of its normative developmentalist character."[299]

A New Concept of the Political

In his account of sovereignty and agonism in the political sphere, Schmitt observes, at one point, how "each participant is in a position to judge whether the adversary intends to negate his opponent's way of life and therefore must be repulsed or fought *in order to preserve one's own form of existence.*"[300] According to Schmitt, liberal politics failed because their reliance on procedure led to depoliticization of the political world. Following Nietzsche, Schmitt argues that the task of the state, in recuperating the political, is to go beyond an abstract ethical universalism – to go *beyond good and evil* –arguing that liberalism is an historical event that brought certain ideas of individual rights and freedoms, but also ideas related to structures of power and domination that afforded colonialism's hatred of the Other. Schmitt makes the argument that because it serves *all*, state liberalism is not neutral. His key contribution, then, may be his deconstruction of the liberal Lockean/Hegelian vision that the state could be grounded in some form of consensus or use of reason. Instead, Schmitt contends, that *all* forms of political authority are grounded in violence, and that although liberal political orders, in particular, seek to cover this over, the traces of this inherent violence are increasingly gaining visibility.

On the question of sovereignty, Schmitt argues that, "if a people no longer possesses the energy or the will to maintain itself in the sphere of politics, the latter will not thereby vanish from the world. Only a weak people will disappear."[301] For him the concept of the state presupposes the political,[302] and sovereignty is the political status of an organized people over an enclosed territorial unit. Schmitt's critique of liberalism centers on liberalism's attempt to depoliticize political thought, as "today nothing is more modern than the onslaught against the political [...] There must no longer be political problems, only organizational-technical and economic-sociological ones."[303]

For Schmitt, a pacified state implies the evacuation of politics, but likewise, the possibility of war is a presupposition that creates a specific political behavior. Schmitt, invoking a Hobbesian argument, writes, "what always matters is the possibility of the extreme case taking place, the real war, and the decision whether this situation has or has not arrived."[304] In Schmitt's book on Hobbes, he writes, "the mechanization of the conception of the State has ended by bringing about the mechanization of the anthropological understanding of human beings."[305] A passion for the real thus appears to be Schmitt's driving impulse: "for only in real combat is revealed the most extreme consequence of the political grouping of friend and enemy. From this moment of "extreme possibility," he concludes, "human life derives its specifically political tension."[306] To put it succinctly, for Schmitt it is only in these exceptional circumstances that the true nature of the state can be revealed.

Schmitt's argument provides the impetus, yet is the conservative double of Mouffe and Laclau's socialist critique in *Return of the Political,* of liberal humanism and its tendency to depoliticize through formal systems of deliberation. Considering that we have identified the stakes in ecology today, they are equally attempts to overcome the instrumentalization of ethics, democracy, and economics, namely, liberal-humanist modes of circulation serving as the basis of contemporary democratic materialism. Schmitt's diagnoses provide an intriguing framework through which to critically perceive the question of ecology and its challenges to sovereignty today – and, ultimately, its relation to the limits of liberal politics, albeit with some notable and problematic reservations – including Schmitt's own odious politics.

For Schmitt, the notion of *the political* has four features:

- The concept of the state presupposes the concept of the political;
- The political precedes the state;
- The political is a basic characteristic of human life;
- The affirmation of the political is the affirmation of the state of nature.[307]

For Schmitt, the question of the sovereign and the political reveals the case of *extremis necessitas casus*—that is, the exception. Within the exception, is the formation of an immanent political truth for Schmitt, as he writes,

> The exception is more interesting than the rule. The rule proves nothing; the exception proves everything: It confirms not only the rule but also its existence, which derives only from the exception. In the exception the power of real life breaks through the crust of a mechanism that has become torpid by repetition.[308]

Schmitt's theoretical work is emblematic of a fidelity to Hobbes and a specific investigation attempting to understand the meaning of excess in the Great Game of global politics, as well as its fragmented assembly of power, territory, jurisdiction and sovereignty. In his enthusiasm to find ultimate truths in a state of exceptional excess, Schmitt calls forth the exception as 'nihilist utopia' and, as previously stated, a passion for the real. In Schmitt's work is a theory of structural formation, however, without an analysis of the irreducibility of the desiring subject as such.

Theory of the Ecological Partisan

Schmitt argues that irregular, partisan warfare in Europe was known since the 18th century. In his analysis, "the theory of the partisan flows into the question of the real enemy and of a new nomos of the earth,"[309] beginning in the modern period with the Spanish resistance to French occupation from 1808-13.[310] One of the innovations of Napoleonic war, Schmitt observes, was "partisan warfare on a grand scale."[311]

From Mao's perspective, it was Lenin who provided a political framework for the term "partisan warfare."[312] For both, there were three characteristics that defined the partisan: The partisan was of a telluric character; s/he took a defensive posture; and s/he was an irregular fighter. A distinction also emerged between defensive and globally aggressive, revolutionary partisans. In Lenin's idea of the revolutionary, "war becomes global civil war and ceases to be interstate war,"[313] Schmitt writes, further pointing out how, for Mao and Lenin, the only just war was a revolutionary war.[314] Schmitt's analysis includes consideration of how Mao and Lenin brought politics into spatial ordering in a new revolutionary mode of orientation.

From the *Swiss Everyman's Guide to Guerilla Warfare* to Mao's strategic discussions in his theoretical work, there exists a rich body of literature related to questions of strategies and tactics of guerilla, or partisan warfare. Schmitt identifies some characteristics of guerilla warfare in his own work; for example, that there is a limited nature of hostility and a spatial configuration relying on an autochthonous population. This type of partisan fighter is characterized by four specific features: irregularity, increased mobility, intensity of political engagement, and telluric character.[315] International law, on the other hand, has a tendency of viewing the conduct of war based primarily on the state and a bracketing of war.[316] Bracketing of wars became a phenomenon in the 18th century as part of a new Westphalian framework.[317] With this invention of a customary legal framework, the notion of a *just war* emerged out of predominantly ideological beginnings.

The idea of the partisan from the nineteenth to the twentieth centuries took on many forms. The Prussian edict of 1813 obliged citizens to resist the invading enemy.[318] Hegel's dialectic, coincidentally, constructed a systematic mediation between tradition and revolution in the early 19th century.[319] For Lenin, a partisan was part of analyzing the concrete situation—a purely tactical or strategic question.[320] It was a question of understanding absolute war that was based on absolute enmity. With the formation of alliances and extra-nation-state bodies in the 20th Century (like NATO, for example), the phenomenon of *Grossräumen*, large spatial-political spheres, emerged.[321] For Schmitt, the phenomenon of the partisan gives rise to the development of a *rigorous enmity*, wherein we have a continuation of politics by other means, but a means that ultimately subsumes politics.

The *nomos* of the earth confronts us with the question of whether partisan warfare can be bracketed and regulated. Had partisan warfare only been a tactical strategy of war, it would merely have been part of the science of war; however, according to Schmitt, the revolutionary war made it into something of a world historical character.[322] Through this lens, Schmitt also identified the possibly of new planetary dimensions of sovereignty:

> Technical-industrial progress makes possible the journey into cosmic spaces, and thereby opens up equally immeasurable new possibilities for political conquests, because the new spaces can and must be appropriated by men. Old-style land-and-sea appropriations, as known in the previous history of mankind, will be followed by new-style space-appropriations.[323]

The partisan was a subject of study, not just for Schmitt. For Che Guevera, "the partisan is the Jesuit of war."[324] In Clausewitz's writings on war, there is an assumption of the regularity of the state. Crucially for Schmitt, the partisan is the consequence of the denial of real enmity and its attempted subsumption within the processes of liberal democracy. Schmitt writes, "only the denial of real enmity paves the way for the destructive work of absolute enmity."[325] This distinction between real enmity and absolute enmity is, for Schmitt, what produces a disaster. In his view, "today there is a crisis of law, thus also a crisis of legality."[326] Schmitt argues that new types of enmity "will produce new unexpected forms of a new partisan,"[327] adding that "the theory of the partisan flows into the question of the real enemy and of a new nomos of the earth." [328]

What Schmitt brings to the question of ecology today, is the old enquiry into the legitimacy of sovereignty and of the customary/actual laws that govern the world. In the context of the Anthropocene and the high stakes it entails, the bracketing of war, as well as the dividing up of land, sea, and air are once again open questions brought to visibility by the potential of global scarcity and cataclysm on the horizon. The Indian writer, Arundathi Roy reminds us:

> The first step towards reimagining a world gone terribly wrong would be to stop the annihilation of those who have a different imagination – an imagination that is outside of capitalism and communism. An imagination which has an altogether different understanding of what constitutes happiness and fulfillment. To gain this philosophical space, it is necessary to concede some physical space for the survival of those who may look like the keepers of our past, but who may really be the guides to our future. [329]

Geopolitical Nomos

Geopolitics is an attempt at a meta-comprehension of a world system of global spatial politics; the underlying dynamics of power in the global theatre; and its contestations of control and coercion. The political order also falls within the geopolitical order. As Schmitt writes in *The Nomos of the Earth*:

No sooner had the form [*Gestalt*] of the earth emerged as a real *globe* [*Globus*]—not just sensed as myth, but apprehensible as fact and measurable as space—than there arose a wholly new and hitherto unimaginable problem: the spatial ordering of the entire earth [*Erdenballes*] in terms of international law. The new global image [*globale Raumbild*] required a new global spatial order. This was the situation resulting from the circumnavigation of the earth and the great discoveries of the 15th and 16th centuries, required a new spatial order. Thus began the epoch of modern international law that lasted until the 20th century.[330]

Endemic to the interactions between humanity and Nature are the markings of territory, spatial orderings and the production of spaces through given apparatuses. The work of Henri Lefebvre and Foucault push such ideas further, opening up a much more coherent and critical understanding of the metabolic production of space under the law of the state and capital. Foucault writes that "sovereignty is exercised within the borders of a territory, discipline is exercised on the bodies of individuals, and security is exercised over a whole population."[331] Foucault further defines the important concept of *biopower*. As he writes in *Security, Territory, Population*:

a number of phenomena that seem to me to be quite significant, namely, the set of mechanisms through which the basic biological features of the human species became the object of a political strategy, of a general strategy of power, or, in other words, how, starting from the eighteenth century, modern western societies took on board the fundamental biological fact that human beings are a species. This is roughly what I have called biopower.[332]

Lefebvre, in his important work *The Production of Space*, is concerned with the formation of space over time and the relations revealed throughout that process. He writes, "what we are concerned with, then, is the long *history of space*, even though space is neither a 'subject' or an 'object' but rather a social reality—that is to say, a set of relations and forms."[333] In Ecological Metapolitics, there is a localized *activation* and *world-making* that materially produces the world and creates a subject as a consequence of the event, in an act of creative novelty and political invention. Without an event that can open up a novel sequence for a new world, our current asymmetrical and metabolic interaction between humanity and Nature will stay *as it is*—the consequences of which might result in what Agamben refers to as the continuation of the "camp as the biopolitical *nomos* of the planet." [334]

Nature belonged to the world before human existence, but the emergence of humanity into the world resulted in its emergence as a part *of* Nature. This relation between humanity and Nature is a metabolic interaction of consequences—a wager of either the finite or the infinite as a material construction. The exceptional status of humanity in relation to other species, as we have discussed, lies in its capacity to destroy the world of the living and non-living, not just over time, but instantaneously. There is also a singularity to global warming as its scale and complexity are more existentially drastic than is the case with other environmental crises. It impacts the entire human collective, though it does so not equally, but asymmetrically. As a consequence of this new truth in the field of science, universal truths will emerge as an ordeal of the subjectivized body, a body beyond Westphalian logics, a body constituting *bare life*.

Global Power, Spatial Ordering

Global power relations, whether between nation-states or between global actors situated within capital, comprise a rubric of strategies and tactics over the control of space and power under the names, *geopolitics* and *geostrategy*. These words have historically functioned on the side of the imperial aims of nation-states and continue to constitute an internal rhetorical world for the exertion of power in global space over time. There are burning questions to consider: How will environmental change effect global power relations? How will this change be applied, articulated and disseminated within the field of geostrategy (historically a discourse of the state concerning the assertion of strategic power at a global or regional scale)? What are the implications of these strategies, tactics, and techniques of power, that function at a global level, and how are they localized? Finally, what are the proper philosophical questions we can construct from these real-world situations?

As anthropogenic climate change develops and the planet warms over the century, establishing ever-accelerating feedback loops that may be irreversible, it is virtually impossible to predict the actual impact of climate change in any definitive fashion. Existential uncertainty and anxiety are built into these questions of ecology, and we assume a loss-of-control over the future as a result of that uncertainty. Droughts, hurricanes, floods, food and water shortages, and other extreme weather events will also lead to mass displacements of peoples. Planning for a state of permanent chaos becomes a self-fulfilling prophecy.

These strategic planning documents also open up an argument for greater expenditures in military equipment and personnel to address the threats of so-called resource wars. New terms arrive such as *food security*, *climate refugees*, *green development*, *resilience*, and so on, but if the primary purpose of the state has become the maintenance of order, the apparatus that supports this function has become tactically more sophisticated and expansive through the use of new technologies that accelerate processes of governmentality, including strategies of hyper-surveillance. Ulrich Beck makes the argument that what has emerged is something called the "risk society," discursively altering the subjective stance from "I am hungry" to "I am afraid."[335]

The investment by states in the mass surveillance of their own citizens is unprecedented, as we have come to see in the situations exposed by Wikileaks, and the various clandestine activities of the National Security Agency (NSA) in the United States. Security apparatuses in other states also reveal a marked expansion of similar activities, echoing Agamben's sentiment that *we are all homo sacer*. Design theorist Benjamin Bratton argues that there is an emerging transformation in the always, already given relationship between governance and technology that is retooling sovereignty at a global scale:

> Our interest is not so much design at a geopolitical scale, rather to take the geopolitical architecture we have inherited from the Treaty of Westphalia, from Empires past, etc. and to literally take the world map

as an open design question once again...We're looking at planetary scale computation as a force that represents a long-term challenge to the world map.[336]

Since the beginning of this century, the state as both object and process is undergoing a crisis of legitimacy, such that the maintenance of order has become its prime directive. The underside of power and its activities remain officially unacknowledged and without visibility; the deep state lurks below. What we have today is the material arrival of *hyperobjects* and their anxious, almost unreceivable, reception within an inoperative community.[337] The task is to bring into cultural legibility a politics of Nature, or a politics of the non-human: a *politics without a referee,* as Bruno Latour refers to it to challenge the inertia of democratic materialism.

The techniques of resistance need to be reformulated, reconfigured, reassembled, and invented again due to the challenges against spontaneous organization presented by the prevalence of mass surveillance in the contemporary world. The modes of technology that promise moments of liberation and rhizomatic, spontaneous intervention into the political space, have become the very devices of control that limit the potential of political scale, and the power of politics to produce ruptures and antagonisms. This is the double bind. There is not really a tension between security and human rights as the state itself has superimposed the limit point and definitions of acceptability on to these terms, within its own internal logics and schematics – in a sense defining what security is and what human rights are, almost unilaterally. Arendt's critique of *the right to have rights* is grounded in the very form of sovereignty against which those rights are invoked.

The prominent geo-strategist Zbigniew Brzezinksi, former U.S. National Security Advisor, acknowledges the expansion of instantaneous surveillance in his writing as early as 1970:

The technotronic era involves the gradual appearance of a more controlled society. Such a society would be dominated by an elite, unrestrained by traditional values. Soon it will be possible to assert almost continuous surveillance over every citizen and maintain up-to-date complete files containing even the most personal information about the citizen. These files will be subject to instantaneous retrieval by the authorities.[338]

Brzezinski also reveals the ideological bias behind the imperial thinking of the major powers in defining the intent behind geostrategy and geopolitics in this way:

> To put it in a terminology that harkens back to the more brutal age of ancient empires, the three grand imperatives of imperial geostrategy are to prevent collusion and maintain security dependence among the vassals, to keep tributaries pliant and protected, and to keep the barbarians from coming together.[339]

State-driven and market-driven capitalism begin to resemble one another as a vulgar double on the global scale, wherein repression of the citizenry takes on different scales, modes, and models. But the bio-political dimension and techniques of control are practiced by virtually all states, no matter their political form. Capital needs to circulate and move around for the process of accumulation to take place, with each cyclical economic downturn requiring another layer of policy to be stripped away to create artificial value required by the laws of financialization. Democratic materialism *shape-shifts* as required, to make this process efficient today.

Brzezinski writes about a possible future that includes 'vigilant garrison states' that combine the synthesized features of democracy with authoritarian characteristics. Countries like India, Israel, Singapore, Brazil, and many others have already developed the technological and legal capacity to keep their nations together by force, including repressive legislative conditions while permitting democratic features such as voting, free press, legal procedures and the right to free assembly. This mutation is the movement from the present to the future in most 'democratic' states, if the world maintains a repetition *as it is.*
Brzezinski writes:

The very latest techniques have been harnessed to monitor suspicious movements, access to public (including non-governmental) facilities is carefully controlled, vehicles and individuals are subject to searches, and many citizens carry arms openly for self-protection. Video surveillance, radiological and biochemical monitoring, infrared and electronic systems to detect even rubber rafts along the shores, extensive and technologically sophisticated perimeter zones for vital industries and public services, personal data loaded I.D. cards, proactive penetration of potentially hostile groups, and forceful interrogation techniques that have helped to anticipate and thus to thwart a majority of would-be terrorists.[340]

In his book on the tactics of the Israeli occupation, *Hollow Land: Israel's Architecture of Occupation*, architectural theorist Eyal Weizman has highlighted how the reading lists of military institutions rely on post-colonial and post-structuralist theory, from philosophers such as Deleuze and Guattari. By adjusting the Israeli military's tactics in urban zones towards deterritorialization and non-linearity, these strategies are now circulating and *in vogue* with security establishments in other countries. In his interview with Weizman, former co-director of the Israel Defense Forces' Operational Theory Research Institute, Shimon Naveh states:

Although so much is invested in intelligence, fighting in the city is still incalculable and messy. Violence makes events unpredictable and prone to chance. Battles cannot be scripted. Command cannot have an overview. Decisions to act must be based on chance, probability, contingency and opportunity, and these must be taken only on the ground and in real time.[341]

The subsumption of critical theory within the capitalist state logic and security regimes is a function of the state defining what is inside or outside the constitution of the acceptable political terrain. It attempts to appropriate and instrumentalize critical theory in a manner that results in a kind of epistemic violence. The surveillance logic of the state has reconstituted the terrain of struggle on the ground and in the field of theory. In this sense, it is not strange for philosophers such as Howard Caygill re-reading Clausewitz as a theorist of resistance. A distinct and disturbing cross-reading is happening between grassroots radical activists and military planners; perhaps they will set up reading groups in the not too distant future, and argue over who brings the cheese plate and appetizers to the potluck.

Such a state is emblematic of a neoliberal gesture *par excellence.* Just as we must distrust the terms "political philosophy," "environmental ethics," "democracy," and "human rights," we must also anticipate the ways in which "critical theory" can itself become a distorted simulacrum in the hands of power when placed under the condition of a political programme. There is a desire in philosophy and politics to draw a distinction between real change and repetition of what already is. Geopolitics has given itself the power to define terms, establish systems of classification, and articulate a terrain and architecture of analyzing power into a seemingly objective and hegemonic *lingua franca.* Even with the inevitability of the massive unforeseen changes in the world brought upon by climate change, there will remain concerted efforts to assert global domination by state actors. It is precisely this uncertainty that is being planned for and studied today in research centres, think tanks, and academic/military conferences largely outside of broader public circulation. The task of the political movement of ecology is to bring into visibility this subterranean apparatus that ultimately functions in the underbelly and shadow of state power.

There are geopolitical dimensions in every region impacted by global warming. As the Arctic Sea ice melts, who will define and control the new waterways and legitimate access to resource extraction from the newly accessible ocean floor? Just as in previous eras where the Panama Canal and the Suez Canal were the sites of geopolitical drama as potential chokepoints for the transportation needs of the capitalist economic system, so too will the new waterways in the Arctic be a site of intense global contestation. In sub-Saharan Africa, existing linguistic, ethnic and sectarian conflicts will be exacerbated by the impacts of global warming, particularly its impacts on access to food and water. The question of Nature, of anthropogenic climate change, demands a human response to this crisis of the possibility of a future by changing the world today. The technology to maintain domination over Nature and space will not only rapidly change, but will accelerate, generating new questions of sovereignty in its wake. Marxist literary critic Fredric Jameson writes that information flow will challenge sovereignty in new ways, stating that, "information is the new element that reproblematizes the spatial."[342]

In the world of geopolitics, in every epoch without exception, including the present period of the *Great Acceleration*, the Great Game *is* the Spirit of the Age. Inscribed within the language of geopolitics is the propaganda of power and where you see its true face unfold. In the design of this future, the state authorizes a trace from above that sets the limit point of the possibility of change within a given horizon. It is against this scope and this inscription by the state of the limits of political possibility and political time that philosophy must speak in its own name, inscribing its own countersignature as part of an affirmative dialectic.

Nomos of the (Post) Anthropocene

Benjamin Bratton argues that the age of planetary scale computation will shift geopolitical sovereignty to create some other known political geography in its post-Westphalian wake. Such a shift will create partitions, brackets, and demands from the citizen-subject on how sovereignty can ultimately be redesigned. Another world is possible, but in its anticipation, what is the nature of the opening to come? What Bratton calls planetary scale computation, networks and geoscapes are fabricated and entered into. They contain jurisdictions, territories, and, what he calls 'stacks'. Interventions in the world are both a remedy and a poison. Place must be re-established in this radically decentered vision, a kind of hallucination of the future. This "accelerationist escape" proposes to design a project of a *projected ethics* of the *not yet*. In so doing, it aims to reformulate a geopolitical ontology. What Bratton calls "nomos of the cloud" is thus a substrate of the geopolitical order of Schmitt's "nomos of the earth."[343]

For Bratton, the old *nomos* of the earth was a "sweeping topological accounting of territorial interpellation of the Greek and Roman worlds, divided and partitioned territories defining logics of sovereignty."[344] The Westphalian logic proposed the making of a territorial order through the state, within which we find the subdivisions of territory containing a form of arbitrary capture and where each break contained a particular *nomo*

For Bratton, the event is an historically original production of a new conceptual superstructure, an active moment of the constitutive. Bratton argues that the encounter with the new world led to the movement from free soil to the European jurisdictional margins of the Treaty of Westphalia. Today, the emergence of planetary-scale computation is a challenge to the existing geopolitical order that is a residue of Westphalian logic. The relationship to the air further problematizes the spatial—drone warfare being a contemporary example of just such a problematic relating to technology, the air, spatial organization and international law.

Bratton proposes a "nomos of the modern" to describe the suspension of the juridical order to create a "spatial exception" that "interweave[s] [the] thickened landscape of territorial claims."[345] He describes such a nomos of the modern, as a mega-structure that perforates and distorts, and where new technologies produce novel territories in their own image to the emergence of hyperbolic forms of governmentality. Bratton proposes the question, what is the new and how does it construct its apparatus? There are layers and protocols implicit in the form. There is a dialectic between equilibrium and emergence. Within this compossible metastructure we find germinations of disruptive contaminations of the biopolitical order. This predominance of new modes proposes an escape from the final sovereignty of the state, wherein this emergence is a possibility of new forms of agonism that are beyond the layers of sovereign claims.

Bratton asks, what are the challenges to thought that the *projected ethics* of the *not-yet* demand? He argues for a geopolitics of addressability to name, organize, and spatialize, a reordering within a sequence, and for the creation of new concepts and logics to find a new executable code and a quantification of sets. For Bratton, this *projected ethics* of the *not-yet* is an augmented reality mediated by a set of technologies that are irredeemably, a cult; there is a subtitling of clean and unclean.[346] This respatializing is a displacing of the traditional Renaissance model of the state and sovereignty that relied upon the fiction of anthropocentrism and a plasticity of the world. Bratton argues that what we have before us is a "design-like situation" that is a premeditation to project and enforce that projection, as *a reaction* and *in relation to* an emergency.[347] In this geopolitical vision, ecology is reinvented at a planetary scale, coupled with the invention of languages for non-human actors. They are numbered and named, *to be counted as the one,* and put together to *form a set.* Critically, in this reordered condition exists the desire to locate the sovereign within the political and to determine what we want from these technologies. Central to this question of redesign, is the fundamental, affirmative question, namely, what are post-Anthropocene and post-Westphalian logics?[348]

There must be a determination of what is or is not reducible to politics. Bratton's new conception of sovereignty multiplies borders into multi-jurisdictional enclaves, redrawing demarcations of inclusion and exclusion in counter-mapping scenarios, forecasting twitches deployed through rhetorics. New technologies build new tools, and the question we ought to be asking in the post-Anthropocene, according to Bratton, is what is to be accelerated? In the deep time of media, Bratton argues that there is *phonic disequilibria.* In the process of destroying the end time it is imperative to know time *for whom* and *for what.*[349] Bratton proposes thinking and designing with chaos, trauma, disruption, and speculative agendas for the "invention of a new kind of accident."[350] By better understanding the set of technologies and objects in the world, there will be new forms, new maps of geography and new geologic eras. Bratton argues that the contemporary period is shaped by modernism, inertia, and fundamentalism.

Ultimately Bratton's proposal is to move beyond what he calls "instrumental prosthetics" to a post-humanism that contemplates planetarity and its incompleteness with an inventory of contingencies and an index of effects of the unresolveable. Planetary contemplation includes local traces and degraded effects, pushing Bratton to argue that computation as style of thought, subtracted from its contemporary economic instrumentality, proposes the possibility of new political architectures. This type of "accelerationist aesthetics" is an "indulgence in imagining without reserve the world-without-us-to-come [and] presumes huge sums of general catastrophe and stares straight down the rabbit hole."[351] The *apophenia* caused by this disorientation sees patterns in the noise. The post-human idea within ecology is concerned with the question of what will succeed and exceed capitalism, proposing a displacement of the human agent resulting in "alienation from history and anthropocentric time and scale."[352] It is a rupture of the circulatory system of the *zombie-body* of anthropocentric capitalism. This speculative posturing requires proper telescoping and prototyping, generative of a new relation to sovereignty. As Hobbes presciently observed: "state and revolution, leviathan and behemoth, are actually or potentially always present," and "the leviathan can unfold in unexpected historical situations and move in directions other than those plotted by its conjurer."[353] Bratton concedes that we must acknowledge the reductions and losses that come with modelization. Accelerationism, at its worst moments, is a flirtation with nihilism and sets out *encounter traps*.

Accelerationism within ecology could also be seen as an attempt to bring about the real state of emergency. As Walter Benjamin observed, "The tradition of the oppressed classes teaches us that the 'state of emergency' in which we live is the rule. We must attain to a concept of history that is in keeping with this insight. Then we shall clearly realize that it is our task to bring about the real state of emergency."[354] Bratton's newly redesigned sovereignty ushers in the possibility of a new citizen-subject. Each historical break of a *nomos* produces an historically original production of a new legal superstructure. As Jameson argues, it reproblematizes the spatial. This new "nomos of the cloud," through the prototype of the stack that describes features of "a possible new nomos of the earth linking technology, nature and the human," produces new territories in its own image through formal and informal violences.[355] This geopolitics of the moment is knotted by the myriad violences of the stack, and the anterior stratum of crowds and power. It becomes the task of philosophy to distinguish between events and pseudo-events. The stack is territorializing or deterritorializing, depending on its relation to the state. Bratton argues that this relation between equilibrium and emergence is the work of the architects to come.[356]

The provision and incomplete networks built on the cloud and stacks overcome the traditional sovereignty of the state, overlapping and interweaving without international jurisdiction. This geography of sovereignty, Bratton explains, includes the policing of one's own breaching. These massively distributed technologies that connect people and things, escape the final sovereignty of the state. Bratton argues that struggles for control of meta-categoricalization will shape the ideological battlefield. This new sovereignty will be simultaneously of the ill and the good, and may require backcasting to determine the ethics of these emergences after the fact. According to Bratton, by determining which emergency we should address, it will be possible to consider radical transformative design on a large scale. For Bratton, design as designation determines in advance what it projects and then enforces that projection. In this sense design can redefine the political and the social. Concretely speaking, Bratton predicts the emergence of languages that represent non-human actors and a force of law of the inanimate. For Bratton, the task of philosophy is to locate the sovereign within the political as a new site of contestation, taking into account the effects of expansive information technology on decentering traditional concepts of sovereignty. Making a case for delinking global systems in favour of smaller, localizable ecologies and subdivisions of sovereignty, Bratton proposes a post-Anthropocene alternative platform that has the command of a plan with the improvised order of the network. There is an epistemology of transactions that produces accumulative accidents. What needs to be determined is what *is* or *is not* determined by the polis, by redrawing boundaries of exclusions and inclusions or, as Schmitt observes, determining who is friend and who is not, actively determining where politics is located and for whom.[357]

The post-Anthropocene, post-capitalist world is an attempt to overcome the architecture of the 19th-century humanist vision. As Paul Virilio has observed, there is a confusion of global speed with local flux. The proposition is to define and put into practice the future alterity through a fidelity to the event, as a speculative agenda accounting for meta-transformations. It is the invention of a new kind of accident outside national territorial waters and the capacities of the nation-state. This augmented reality proposes a new, designable event. For Bratton, it is a movement "rooted in precarity of globalizations as irresolveable as they are interconnected."[358]

Human experience should be tilted off-centre. Bratton concedes that "we are attentive to how planetary-scale computation's instrumentalization of Design to model its political arrivals also provides aesthetic' programs which are less reflective of political realities than generative of their material evolution." Bratton argues that, "it is necessary to retrain the work of the 'political' away from a direct confrontation with or acceleration of Capitalism *as the scope of the problem as such,* and instead towards a direct engagement-in-advance of what exceeds it."[359] 'Post-Anthropocene,' as a term, appeals to Bratton over 'post-Capitalism' because the former "not only names another eco-economic order but articulates in advance the displacement of the human agent from the subjective center of its operations." It requires a mature alienation "from human history and anthropocentric time and scale."[360]

The spatial sphere of influence moves beyond territorial claims to something else. Spatial supremacy is constructed in new ways, disrupting the medieval notion of *Rex est imperator in regno suo*—that the king is ruler within his own kingdom. For Bratton, within the movement towards the post-Anthropocene, "one of the first things to dissolve is perhaps the coherency of any normative *polis* or *polity*…the representable political body doesn't endure long enough for its polity to take shape," he writes, and "…that failure may be the key accomplishment of accelerationist "politics" as an epistemology of design."[361] A new theory of political geography beyond terrestrial space emerges, or as Bratton argues, "The accident also produces a new technology." [362]

Though Badiou and Bratton's work is incongruous and openly contradictory when looked at together, to adequately scope the movement from the present to the future in relation to the question of ecology today, they can be productively read together as providing competing conceptual frameworks for the construction of the new, regarding the human relation to political invention in the Anthropocene. We must, however, be skeptical of the problem of ecology being presented exclusively as a problem of design. What, today, often goes by the name of 'design thinking' is, more often than not, a continuation of a market logic of value creation dressed up in a new language. It traditionally operates on the side of the incumbents of power.

Quentin Meillassoux, in his book: *After Finitude: An Essay on the Necessity of Contingency,* calls for philosophy to help us *"to get out of ourselves,* to grasp the in-itself, to know what is whether we are or not."[363] The 'ancestral' he defines as the time before human existence that can be articulated with scientific proofs that are revisable through method. He defines, as an example, some empirical facts of the ancestral:

- the date of the origin of the universe (13.5 billion years ago)
- the date of the accretion of the earth (4.56 billion years ago)
- the date of origin of life on earth (3.5 billion years ago)
- the date of the origin of humankind *(Homo habilis,* 2 million years ago)[364]

Additionally, there are four long-term spikes related specifically to the Anthropocene in areas such as "population growth, consumption of resources, carbon gas emissions, and the mass extinction of species." [365]

That the world exists before us and that this remains in the realm of the thinkable as a task of philosophy disrupts the question of ecology—and of being itself—substantially. It returns us to the basic philosophical questions *What do I know?*, and, *What should I do*? There has been already a world without us and could be again a future without us. According to Meillassoux, for philosophy to adequately speculate into the future as a form of thinking, there needs to be an acknowledgement of certain knowledges that have been overlooked in the mode of thinking philosophy. Speculative realism is also a novel intervention to reconsider the understanding of the metabolic relation between humanity and Nature in light of the Anthropocene whether we are or not.

In the relation between science and continental philosophy, Catherine Malabou asks, 'can we relinquish the transcendental?,' and can we remain in the continental tradition? The world, after all, is capable of existing without us. It exists before human and philosophical colonization. The world as it is, is radically contingent. Within speculative realism is movement decentering the Anthropocentric by proposing a new relation between science and continental philosophy related to being as such – it is a call for a new idea of the transcendental in opposition to Kant, in light of science. The world cannot be guaranteed *a priori*. Anything might happen, maybe nothing at all. The prophet overthrew the king. [366]

Accelerationism and its Discontents

Accelerationism, the historical Marxian sense, is the belief that capitalism should be expanded and sped up so that its contradictions, crises, and self-destructive tendencies will arrive sooner. For the Accelerationists, the Anthropocene is the Long March to a post-human trace. As Marx himself writes in, "On the Question of Free Trade":

> But, in general, the protective system of our day is conservative, while the free trade system is destructive. It breaks up old nationalities and pushes the antagonism of the proletariat and the bourgeoisie to the

extreme point. In a word, the free trade system hastens the social revolution. It is in this revolutionary sense alone, gentlemen, that I vote in favor of free trade.[367]

Here Marx was trying to bring about the social revolution in his qualified gesture of consent to the notion of free trade. Deleuze and Guattari, by comparison, write in *Capitalism and Schizophrenia* that accelerationism is the revolutionary direction:

> Which is the revolutionary path?...To withdraw from the world market?...Or might it be to go in the opposite direction? To go still further, that is, in the movement of the market?...Not to withdraw from the process," they wager, "but to go further, to accelerate the process.[368]

Nick Land projects that the acceleration of capitalism and its technological extensions would lead to "effectively experiencing a species-wide suicide as the ultimate stimulant head rush."[369] Alex Williams argues that accelerationism is a strategy to overcome the inevitable closures that present themselves when critique is presented of capitalism or neo-liberalism as such:

> what becomes crucial is the ability of a reconstituted Left to not simply operate inside the hegemonic coordinates of the possible as established by our current socioeconomic setup. To do so requires the ability to direct preexisting and at present inchoate desires for post-capitalism towards coherent visions of the future. Necessarily, given the experimental nature of such a reconstitution, much of the initial labor must be around the composition of powerful visions able to reorient populist desire away from the libidinal dead end which seeks to identify modernity as such with neoliberalism, and modernizing measures as intrinsically synonymous with neoliberalizing ones (for example, privatization, marketization, and outsourcing). This is to invoke the idea, initially coined by Land's Cybernetic Cultural Research Unit, of *hyperstition*—narratives able to effectuate their own reality through the workings of feedback loops, generating new sociopolitical attractors.[370]

Reza Negarestani argues for an "overcoming of anthropomorphism and human arrogance with a negation of the special status of the human and the capacities of reason."[371] Italian activist and theorist Franco "Bifo" Berardi argues that at a time when even our subconscious has been colonized by capitalism, we need strategies to overcome this parasitic attack:

> The reciprocal implication of desire and capitalist development can be properly understood through the concept of schizo deterritorialization. But when it comes to the process of the recomposition of subjectivity and the formation of social solidarity, acceleration implies the submission of the Unconscious to the globalized machine.[372]

The machine of capital and its statist policy not only captures the body but also the unconscious, so the act of decolonization must surpass this level of intrusion. For Berardi, we must storm the heavens and conquer death. This quelling of death was the singular and unrelenting task presented by Nikolai Fedorov—to launch a collective assault on mortality, understood to be part of the human submission to Nature. Fedorov's idea outlines the *duty* for a struggle against death.[373]

The possibility of a misanthropic nihilism designed to create the opening of the new Idea is built into accelerationism. Beyond the linguistic and artistic creation of such a call, is the inability to carry out its demand. The same critique could be leveled at the Left in general. As Gene Moreno writes:

> Accelerationism aims to rev up crisis and render it unsustainable, to pipe even more energy into processes of social fracture, to exacerbate the fragmentation of experience, and to intensify sensorial overload and subjective dispersal in order to drive masochistically toward an incompatibility between capitalism and forms of excess it can't accommodate.[374]

In this technical and utopian claim of the time after the collapse of capitalism, perhaps there will be something less boisterous, even less joyous, on the other side. Lipovetsky acknowledges that the potential end of one system is not to be mistaken with utopia:

> We know very well that as soon as they are destroyed, a new appara-
> tus of power, with a new terror, will replace the old one; but on this
> occasion unbearable reactions are deactivated, others unprecedented,
> sometimes delicious ones become possible, pending the unforeseeable
> moment when they too join the sorrow of the old ones. So that all there
> is for us to do, to hope for, is to cut short the reign of powers and their
> repression, and to do so endlessly, since the combat against powers has
> no end. It's not much, yet it's enormous. Such is the meaning of *perma-
> nent revolution*, which we now identify with the multiple movements
> of acceleration in their desire for a *saving of time*.[375]

Accelerationism thus aligns philosophical thought with capitalist culture in an immanent frame that can speak to the future as, simultaneously, apocalypse and *tabula rasa*. Patricia Reed, while acknowledging its attempt to open up new conceptual space, further critiques the *Accelerationist Manifesto* on several fronts:

> The admirable futural will that drives the Manifesto seems peculiarly
> tentative towards the future. It feels locked in the past on several points,
> looking backwards over its shoulders to recount exemplary precedents
> (largely failed cybernetic ones), self-assured in its nostalgic distance
> and unwilling to take that speculative leap towards the unknown. While
> correctly identifying a certain paralysis that comes over the left when
> faced with the forecasting of alternatives, the Manifesto seems bound
> to its own lamenting diagnosis, unable to prognosticate beyond vague
> assertions…the continued lack or void in fertilizing any sense of be-
> coming possible of the impossible, the articulation of the outside, and
> the production of desire itself.[376]

Reed cites Rousseau's idea of the *artificial soul* as "that which breathes collective life into a political project unbound by axioms of the existent" and as that which requires "fabulation."[377]

Through the surfacing of excess in these investigations, truth procedures emerge that fall inside of the question of ecology today. Badiou's work attempts to reveal or create a subject as a consequence of the event, in a context where political action seems impossible. He does so in a way that leaves out, in the constitution of the subject, the Freudian notion of *death drive*. Badiou's subject comes after Lacan, charting out the generalized, mathematical conditions for transformative action. Accelerationism, too, has a relation to subtraction from the world today and invokes a

speculative possibility for the future that is beyond the interpellation of all things into the neoliberal frame. Accelerationism attempts to leap into the future, driven by the closures of the present,
through a kind of speculative violence that flirts with nihilism. However, by moving into a radically deconsecrated realm of pure speculation in the world that *is not yet,* is also the possibility of the invention of a new idea concerning the present. In a time where the future has been confiscated by experts, it should legitimately be asked, how do we design a collective future inside of Nature? Perhaps the human machine is designed to destroy itself and the earth. In ecology, if we know how to get to the other side, how do we reload the machine?

Like all good fads, Accelerationism in a rather fleeting, nihilistic, but well-intentioned and erudite manner, has some interesting things to say. It takes some targeted shots at the failure of the Left in general (necessary and important work in itself) while speculating on the future in a newly constructed, conceptual sandbox. In its *impotentiality* and *incapacitation,* the discourse succeeds in opening up new registers of understanding and thinking. But, we should caution, it may just be that, for it is also an aesthetic and theoretical decoy that falls under the problem of capital, lacking the political chops for the political claims that it makes, so is predominantly received with energetic and welcome applause within the soft politics inside the monastery of the aesthetic regime as a momentary, fashionable discourse - as fleeting as it is light. It throws down warlike phrases and challenges without having to pay the price, conferring authority from a decadent perch. It may yet be possible to preserve the good intentions of the theoretical excesses embedded within accelerationism – it is, at the very least, an outline of an outside beyond the simplistic remedies of democratic materialism.

There are larges forces at work in the background. As Nietzsche writes, "The time is coming when the struggle for dominion over the earth will be carried on. It will be carried on in the name of fundamental philosophical doctrines." [378]

5

ECOLOGIES OF DESIRE

On Marx's Metabolism

The Darwinian revolution brought to the surface the view that humanity is inescapably a part of Nature, not separate or superior to it - an idea that became an important characteristic of the Enlightenment tradition. In its desire to intervene in the movement from the present to the future, *Ecological Metpolitics* reimagines a new modern tradition for the relation between humanity and Nature. To deconstruct this relationship, for the purposes of reconstructing it again, Marx and Engels are crucial. For both of them, the "antithesis between Nature and history is created" only when "the relation of man to nature is excluded from history."[379] Marx claims that a conception of Nature outside of society is meaningless, as a "nature that preceded human history…today no longer exists anywhere."[380] For Marx, Nature and humanity mediate one another in a metabolic interaction. For Engels,

> Nature becomes dialectical by producing men as transforming, consciously acting Subjects confronting nature itself as forces of nature. Man forms the connecting link between the instruments of labour and the object of labour. Nature is the Subject-Object of labour. Its dialectic consists in this: that men change their own nature as they progressively deprive external nature of its strangeness and externality, as they mediate nature through themselves, and as they make nature itself work for their own purposes."[381]

117

Frankfurt School thinker Alfred Schmidt, however, argues that "the problem of nature, as an object to be mastered, continues to exist,"[382] and suggests that Marx's definition of Nature is at heart, a dialectic of subject and object. More generally, the Frankfurt School analysis of Nature and civilization partially displaces class conflict, with the conflict between human beings and Nature being presented as the motor of history. The Frankfurt School also insists on the relation between the domination of external or sensuous Nature and the domination of human beings over each other via class domination; at both levels, then, class conflict still remains present. Bringing class conflict more centrally into the relation between humanity and Nature, Marxist geographer Neil Smith writes, "Through human labor and the production of nature at the global scale, human society has placed itself squarely at the center of nature."[383] Similarly, Lefebvre argues that "space as a whole has become the place where reproduction of the relations of production is located."[384] For Marx, humanity is not apart from Nature, but is a part of Nature. Through labour, humans produce Nature as part of the creation of a *social Nature*. It is this metabolic interaction that has become distorted since the Enlightenment and the Industrial Revolution. However, since humankind is also the single species that can destroy not only its own existence, but also other species and the natural world at large, there remains an immanent and special relation between Nature and humanity inside the question of ecology that cannot go unaddressed.

In Marx's analysis, we come to know the world by acting in it, and to act in it is to transform it. Any time we transform the world, we alienate ourselves from it. This occurs through social practices, and if there is such a thing as responsibility for the environment, it is necessarily a social one with an orientation toward *social Nature*.[385] As Adorno and Horkheimer express in their work *Dialectic of Enlightenment*, "as its final result, civilization leads back to the terrors of nature."[386]

Marx identifies the perverted capitalist distortion at play between humanity and Nature through its metabolic interaction:

It is not the unity of living and active humanity with the natural, inorganic conditions of their metabolic exchange with nature, and hence their appropriation of nature, which requires explanation or is the result of a historic process, but rather the *separation* between these inorganic conditions of human existence, a separation which is completely posited only in the relation of wage labour and capital.[387]

Over the course of the Enlightenment as a period of technological advances in agriculture especially, came the transition from feudalism to capitalism, from medieval scholasticism to modern science. This disruption in the metabolic exchange of humanity and Nature through technology and labour power, instrumentalized by capital, is the historic backbone of the population expansion and the beginnings of the root causes of accelerated global warming in the present. The period of the post-Enlightenment is the time of unprecedented, exponential human population growth. Marx, in his own time, viewed the situation of the world as a global civil war between Empire and Commune, constituted by a struggle between capital-wage labour and the struggle over surplus-value.

The work of Hegel reveals an understanding of the estrangement of human experience from Nature. Primitive accumulation that occurred in the early stages of capitalism through private property was the beginning of the contemporary dislocation of this relation. The move to private property and its subsequent acceleration through colonialist projects globally drove Engels to observe:

> To make earth an object of huckstering—the earth which is our one and all, the first condition of our existence—was the last step toward making oneself an object of huckstering. It was and is to this very day an immorality surpassed only by the immorality of self-alienation. And the original appropriation—the monopolization of the earth by a few, the exclusion of the rest from that which is the condition of their life—yields nothing in immortality to the subsequent huckstering of the earth.[388]

Assigned to ecological thinking today is the task of making, as Hegel once observed, a revolution out of chaos. Marx referred to this notion of metabolism (brought into philosophy from chemistry and the physical sciences) as *Stoffwechsel*, defined by him as "a process between man and nature, a process by which man and nature, a process by which man, through his own actions, mediates, regulates and controls the metabolism between himself and nature."[389] Marx argues that as a consequence of the human alienation from Nature, there is a need to mediate and govern this metabolic interaction with Nature in a rational way. Marx was looking at the land question through the agricultural revolution and modalities of capitalist expansion that were adjudicating the accelerated disconnection between humanity and Nature:

> Capitalist production collects the population together in great centres, and causes the urban population to achieve an ever-growing preponderance. This has two results. On the one hand it concentrates the historical motive force of society; on the other hand, it disturbs the metabolic interaction between man and the earth, i.e. it prevents the return to the soil of its constituent elements consumed by man in the form of food and clothing; hence it hinders the operation of the natural condition for the lasting fertility of the soil….But by destroying the circumstances surrounding that metabolism…it compels its systematic restoration as a regulative law of social production, and in a form adequate to the full development of the human race…[A]ll progress in capitalist agriculture is a progress in the art, not only of robbing the worker, but of robbing the soil; all progress in increasing the fertility of the soil for a given time is a progress toward ruining the more long-lasting sources of that fertility…Capitalist production, therefore, only develops the technique and the degree of combination of the social process of production by simultaneously undermining the original sources of all wealth…the soil and the worker.[390]

In its essence and historical becoming, capitalism widened the metabolic rift between humanity and Nature. It was not a symbolic cut but a real one that hastened the Great Acceleration. With *Stoffwechsel* representing the material exchange between humanity and Nature, Marx identifies it as having a specific ecological meaning and a social one related to labour:

> Labour is, first of all, a process between man and nature, a process by which man, through his own actions, mediates, regulates and controls the metabolism between him and nature. He confronts the materials of

nature as a force of nature. He sets in motion the natural forces which belong to his own body, his own arms, legs, head and hands, in order to appropriate the materials of nature in a form adapted to his own needs. Through this movement he acts upon external nature and changes it, and in this way he simultaneously changes his own nature.[391]

In this dialectical exchange between humanity and Nature as a metabolic interaction, we find a kernel of a crucial idea in recovering the problem of ecology from the Romantics according to Marx:

Man lives from nature, i.e. nature is his *body,* and he must maintain a continuing dialogue with it if he is not to die. To say that man's physical and mental life is linked to nature simply means that nature is linked to nature, simply means that nature is linked to itself, for man is a part of nature.[392]

This is an argument that ultimately can be attributed to Schelling: that consciousness is nothing other than Nature becoming conscious of itself. This relation between Nature-imposed conditions and the capacity of human beings to affect this process is what is at stake. For Badiou, this movement cannot be done without a movement toward equality, which is ultimately a question of the division of labour and the distribution of wealth. It is this rift in metabolism that is related to the material estrangement between humanity and Nature, for as Marx famously said, the excrement produced by man would need to be returned to the soil in order to complete the metabolic cycle.

Marx insists that even after the revolution, the need to govern the metabolic interaction between humanity and Nature in a rational way would persist. This movement from the world *as it is*, to the metabolic interactions between humanity and Nature is precisely what is in the field of play within *Ecological Metapolitics*. As such, according to Marx, this movement requires the disavowal of two things: the dissolution of humankind's current relation to earth and the dissolution of the currently unequal relations between people. To illustrate this point, he writes:

We know only one science, the science of history. History can be viewed from two sides: it can be divided into the history of nature and that of man. The two sides, however, are not to be seen as independent entities. As long as man has existed, nature and man have affected each other.[393]

Marx's notion of primitive accumulation included, "conquest, enslavement, robbery, murder", whereas for Glen Coulthard, the standard Marxist line of accumulation by dispossession tends to place a focus on the former rather than the latter – a primary distinction between Marxist and indigenous perspectives in defining what constitutes the motor of history.

The Russian revolutionary Nikolai Bukharin, who was arrested and executed on orders by Stalin in the thirties, further developed Marx's ideas of metabolism. Writing from prison, he observed:

> Historical materialism is the fundamental relation between environment and system, between "external conditions" and human society… The metabolism between man and nature consists, as we have seen, in the transfer of material energy from external nature to society… Thus, the interrelation between society and nature is a process of social production. In this process, society applies its human labor energy and obtains a certain quantity of energy from nature ("nature's material," in the words of Marx). The balance *between* expenditures and receipts is here obviously the decisive element for the growth of society. If what is obtained exceeds the loss by labor, important consequences obviously follow for society, which vary with the amount of this excess.[394]

In Bukharin's hands, this idea of metabolic interaction incorporated and developed a movement as the motion of systems in past, present, and future, with Bukharin presenting it as a kind of metabolic flow that is a constant historical project. Within the Marxist project is a materialist ontology of emergence and a notion of embodied time—*mors immortalis*—and, pertinent to the project of *Ecological Metapolitics*, a linking of social transformation with the transformation of the human relation with Nature.

Marx and Engels closely followed the transformation of capitalism, over just a few hundred years, from a phenomenon restricted to a small corner of the world into a totalized world system that specialized in creative destruction:

The bourgeoisie, during its rule of scarce one hundred years, has created more massive and more colossal productive forces than have all preceding generations together. Subjection of nature's forces to man's machinery, application of chemistry to industry and agriculture, steam-navigation, railways electric telegraphs, clearing of whole continents for cultivation, canalization of rivers, whole populations conjured out of the ground. What earlier century had even a presentiment that such forces slumbered in the lap of social labor.[395]

The breaching of boundaries in the exchange between humanity and Nature were collective transgressions. Marx's critique of private property centered on three concepts that were compromised in the process: "a direct relation to nature...the land as a means of production and...a communal relation to the earth."[396] At the heart of this problem, for Marx, was the role of private property in primitive accumulation. Humanity must interact with Nature as part of being, where Marx argues that, "nature is his body, with which he must remain in continuous interchange if he is not to die."[397] It is in this rift of metabolic interaction between humanity and Nature, in other words, that:

[f]or the first time, nature becomes purely an object for humankind, purely a matter of utility; ceases to be recognized as a power for itself; and the theoretical discovery of its autonomous laws appears merely as a ruse so as to subjugate it under human needs, whether as an object of consumption or as a means of production. In accord with this tendency, capital drives beyond national barriers and prejudices as much as beyond nature worship, as well all traditional, confined, complacent, encrusted satisfactions of present needs, and reproductions of old ways of life.[398]

Vitally important to the metabolic relation between humanity and Nature is the human relation to desire, narcissism, and lack – more specifically the relation between capitalism and narcissism. There is also an epistemological violence at the heart of human reasoning that is part of the Enlightenment tradition as a result of its striving for a domination over Nature and non-European peoples. In *On Truth and Lies in a Non-moral Sense,* Nietzsche addresses epistemological violence with the process of seeking to render equal what is unequal. In short the formation of concepts (universals) entails violence against that which is singular. He writes:

> A mobile army of metaphors, metonyms, and anthropomorphisms—in short, a sum of human relations which have been enhanced, transposed, and embellished poetically and rhetorically, and which after long use seem firm, canonical, and obligatory to a people: truths are illusions about which one has forgotten that this is what they are; metaphors which are worn out and without sensuous power; coins which have lost their pictures and now matter only as metal, no longer as coins.[399]

Capitalism subordinates Nature in pursuit of accumulation as its highest value and its tendency to be a totalizing condition. The project of ecology therefore involves reining in the imperial ambitions of thought. There is a choice between explaining or accepting the crisis today as we are now in the realm of an event in both the religious and neo-ecclesiastical sense. In the act of thinking Nature, the current impasse maximizes the power of the subject over the object, where science strips Nature of its enchantment. For Benjamin, "[humankind's] self-alienation has reached such a degree that it can experience its own destruction as an aesthetic pleasure of the first order."[400] As the subject is *itself* object, that is, Nature, it establishes the conditions of its own domination (socially and psychologically; domination and repression respectively).

In a position very much in opposition to Marx, Dipesh Chakrabarty makes a distinction between human and natural histories. He writes: "For it is no longer a question simply of man having an interactive relation with nature. This, humans have always had…Now it is being claimed that humans are a force of nature in the geological sense."[401] For Marcuse, Nature has become a cultural construction mediated through technology. Though humanity and Nature interact with one another, there is a new geological dimension to this relationship in the Anthropocene, that has the potential of apocalypse built into it, for it indicates a process where culture has lost its autonomy and has become instrumentalized. This alienation between technology, Nature and humanity results in a situation where even the possibility of mass catastrophe and spectacle has become a kind of desire for some. The mediating quality of technology, in receiving and disseminating the information flows of catastrophe, has created an estranged relation to empathy in contemporary life, and, as a response, ecology must attempt to recover real life from artificial life, if there is still time.

Marx, has also been cited by today's *Accelerationism* movement. In his piece, *Fragment on Machines,* Marx writes:

> Not as with the instrument, which the worker animates and makes into his organ with his skill and strength, and whose handling depends on his virtuosity. Rather, it is the machine which possesses skill and strength in place of the worker, is itself the virtuoso, with a soul of its own in the mechanical laws acting through it…The worker's activity, reduced to a mere abstraction of activity, is determined and regulated on all sides by the movement of machinery, and not the opposite.[402]

It is also quite possible, in the Žižekian sense, that humanity in relation to Nature is an excremental remainder—a disposable piece of shit. Is the human animal even worth saving? Why does ecology begin with the premise that humanity should be saved – what have we done to deserve that and with what motivations should they justify continued existence? A piece of phenomenological evidence is never a definition, but a path according to Heidegger, beginning with a contrarian nature and including a leap (even if it may end up being wrong), aiming for *irreconcilable distance.* Wolfgang Schirmacher believes that a phenomenological procedure that forces together the ethical with the aesthetic can conflate both in a life technique based on justice, that ultimately appears as *hyperperception.*

Heidegger's term *Gelassenheit* allows for a letting be—by renouncing willing you release yourself to that which is not will. This is the space that allows for noble-minded thinking, for it is prior to the act of thinking. Allowing for an opening, a clearing, is essential to experience *Dasein* (being-there) - the experience of being that is peculiar to human beings. It is a form of being that is aware of and must confront such issues as personhood, mortality and the paradox of living in relationship with other beings, while ultimately being alone with oneself. By resisting the present, the moment can be considered a trace in the dialectic of presence and absence, in a movement from anthropocentrism to anthromorphism. Humans are one of the few species that are not actually required by other species. While we are at least partially dependent on other species, we largely do not contribute to the well-being of other species.

Capital and Nature

Urban geographer David Harvey argues that a dialectic between freedom and domination exists; *ergo*, with the expansion of freedom somewhere, there is domination taking root elsewhere. As he historicizes it: "capital's freedoms clearly rested…on the unfreedom of others."[403] In Adorno's critique of Kant, in the Idealist conception of freedom, these terms go hand-in-hand through the immanent relation of autonomy and legislation. In other words, "I'm free to the extent that I self-legislate and this entails a repression of natural impulse or inclination." Harvey argues that in the field of uneven geographical development, "differentiations in social re-production and in the balance between freedom and domination flourish to the point where they, in themselves, become part of the production of space and uneven development."[404] For Harvey, the metabolic relation between humanity and Nature fall under the problem of capital.

> Capital *is* a working and evolving ecological system within which both nature and capital are constantly being produced and reproduced….The only interesting questions then are: what kind of ecological system is capital, how is it evolving and why might it be crisis prone?[405]

If the relation between humanity and Nature is fixed within the question of capital, it will dominate ecological discourse. For Harvey, "if there are serious problems in the capital-nature relation, then this is an internal contradiction within and not external to capital."[406] Capital's spatial and psychological expansion into the lifeworld of humanity is a central question for Harvey, who further notes the way in which,

[c]apital cannot help but privatize, commodify, monetize and com-
mercialise all those aspects of nature that it possibly can. Only in this
way can it increasingly absorb nature into itself to become a form of
capital—an accumulation strategy—all the way down into our DNA.
This metabolic relation necessarily expands and deepens in response
to capital's exponential growth…The colonization of our lifeworld by
capital accelerates. The endless and increasingly mindless exponential
accumulation of capital is accompanied by an endless and increasingly
mindless extension of capital's ecology into our lifeworld.[407]

Today's stores of carbon and fossil fuels are the remains of prehistor-
ic creatures from millions of years ago. To keep these remains under-
ground for the future of Nature, is fundamentally a battle with capital. As
Harvey writes, "Capitalism will never fall on its own. It will have to be
pushed."[408] The suggestion by Harvey is not that capitalism is an edifice
like the Berlin Wall that simply needs to be brought down, but meta-
phorically in line with one of Marx's elementary points, that capitalism
is a social relation that is produced and reproduced in and through our
practices.[409] It is this relation that needs to undermined to undo capitalism. Lefebvre asserts that capitalism's survival in the twentieth century
has largely to do with the production of space over time, a particular
repetition that Smith calls *uneven development*, "a concrete process and
pattern of the production of nature under capitalism."[410] It is this relation
between time and space that Lefebvre refers to as *rhythmanalysis*, that
links to what Badiou calls *localization,* referring to how the paradox
of these various situations play out, spatially and temporally within the
specificity of a place. The notion that socio-political contradictions are
realized spatially is a point of convergence between Badiou, Harvey and
Lefebvre, where for Badiou, there are not only bodies and languages but
also localized truths that emerge as a consequence of the event.

Waiting for the Disaster

The question of ecology today addresses collective human civilization as
an object of study and the uncertainty proposed by the existential threat

to living beings and the earth, including the expansion of conflict. Commentators in earlier eras also discussed the possibilities of civilizational collapse, particularly during the two World Wars of the last century. With the calamity of the unprecedented destruction opened up by the First World War, Freud observed that the war,

> broke out and robbed the world of its beauties. It destroyed not only the beauty of the countrysides through which it passed and the works of art which it met on its path, but it also shattered our pride in the achievements of our civilization, our admiration for many philosophers and artists, our hopes of a final triumph over the differences among nations and races...In this way it robbed us of so much that we had loved, and showed us the fragility of much that we had considered stable.[411]

In a similar vein, Walter Benjamin speaks to the era as one in which "[a] generation that had gone to school on a horse-drawn streetcar now stood under the open sky in a countryside in which nothing remained unchanged but the clouds, and beneath these clouds, in a field of force of destructive torrents and explosions, was the tiny, fragile human body."[412]

For Peter Sloterdijk, it is a "deliberate nonawareness of the ontological situation...[that] fuel[s] all forms of rapid living, civil disinterestedness and anorganic eroticism."[413] The question today is bound up with the idea that there is a transgressive threshold that becomes a self-fulfilling prophecy. Sloterdijk defines his theory of spheres as "air conditioning systems in whose construction and calibration, for those living in real coexistence, it is out of the question not to participate. The symbolic air conditioning of the shared space is the primal production of every society."[414] The question of Nature is also concerned with the idea of overcoming the ecstasy of our own time, confronting it with a new logic and developing a critique of Western metaphysics and its colonial dismissal of other non-linear modes of thinking. Sloterdijk, for instance, writes that with "any philosophical diagnosis about the time, you have to take an interest in the management of vision and the economy of illusion in mass culture."[415] Moving beyond the ideological trance and stasis of contemporary anxiety, Sloterdijk calls for lives of experimentation, on a search for a superior code. The overproduction of images and texts become *foam* and contribute to the anthropological and moral blindness of the present time.

Schirmacher asks whether "the voluntary extinguishing of the will to life in ourselves would allow humaneness to triumph over nature. What at first appeared as resignation would then reveal itself to be a successful way out," he suggests—"But can something that looks like collective suicide by the human species be called successful?"[416] There is a need, he adds, to be skeptical of discourses that call for a love of Nature. As Schirmacher writes:

> We ought to be skeptical in philosophy of love of nature in the eco-logical discourse as it takes the same subjective fetish as democracy, equality and so on. We must catapult ourselves in to the orientation of a new existence. Today, everything depends upon the difference between *anthropocentric* and *anthropomorphic*, for it is from this difference that we learn how death technique and life technique show themselves.[417]

Schirmacher argues that philosophical thinking is the only remain-ing way to retain an unprejudiced insight into that which is. The task for philosophy, as such, is to take off the anthropocentric mask of society. In paraphrasing Adorno, Schirmacher observes that meaning and value "have been unmasked as ideology."[418] For Heidegger, being needs the human being in order to "present" [*anwesen*].[419] Heidegger also uses the term *Aletheia*—unconcealedness or a revealing of the truth, and it is with the term *Destruktion* that he articulates a kind of negation to recover the truth when it becomes calcified from time to time:

> If the question of Being is to have its own history made transparent, then this hardened tradition must be loosened up, and the concealments which it has brought about dissolved. We understand this task as one in which by taking the question of Being as our clue we are to destroy the traditional content of ancient ontology until we arrive at those primor-dial experiences in which we achieved our first ways of determining the nature of Being—the ways which have guided us ever since.[420]

It is through Heidegger's sense of *thrownness* (*Geworfenheit*) in the contemporary world that the question of ecology reveals itself to us. Badiou argues that within the paradox of ecology is the problem opened up by the death of God, whereas Heidegger, states that, "only a god can save us":

> philosophy will not be able to effect an immediate transformation of the present condition of the world. This is not only true of philosophy, but of all merely human thought and endeavor. Only a god can save us. The sole possibility that is left for us is to prepare a sort of readiness, through thinking and poeticizing, for the appearance of the god or for the absence of the god in the time of foundering [*Untergang*]; for in the face of the god who is absent, we founder.[421]

For Serres, however, "Since the death of God, all we have left is war." [422]

Mastery Over the Mastery of Nature

Integral to the question of Nature is a taking into account of the destroying of worlds of non-human beings. Heidegger, for his part, denies that non-human beings possess worlds; he suggests, at least, that they are poor in worldhood. As humans increase their power over Nature, they lose more control over it. If we are indeed a *part* of Nature and not *apart* from it, in remaking Nature, in producing Nature, how do we remake ourselves in the act of producing it? The contradictions between overconsumption and underdevelopment reflect a transformation that produces and reproduces inequality. With the increased knowledge of ecological impacts there remains a limited will to change—in essence, what humans experience is a dissonance between their capacity to transform the environment and their lack of control over these processes of change. For Heidegger, Nature is merely a "standing reserve."[423]

Adorno, arguing first against Hegel, makes a case for the reclamation of natural beauty; and secondly, against Kant, when he argues for this reclamation without privileging beauty. It is on these matters where Horkheimer suggests that the Enlightenment regresses to the level of mythology. Reason was born of man's desire to dominate Nature, but for Benjamin, it was the "mastery over the mastery of nature" that was at stake—an unfulfilled task for humanity in "coming to terms with nature."[424] For Serres, "Nature is reduced to human nature, which is reduced to history or reason."[425] Increasingly this divide between history and Nature reveals the widening contradiction between the capacity to master Nature, *Naturbeherrschung*, and our inability to control our relationship to Nature. Within this paradox is an attempt to come to terms with the relationship between humanity and Nature, so although we produce Nature, we are also materially mediated by it—Nature is both materially produced and symbolically constructed. There are limits to the appropriation of Nature, moreover, as it is finite. Under total capitalism, there is the function of time and finitude materializing in the hyper-speed of the Anthropocene. There remains the tension between what Michael Lipscomb calls the "urgency of contemporary environmental discourse with the democratic impulse for considered deliberation."[426]

The recent historical circumstances of the Great Acceleration can be tied to post-Second World War economics and its bringing to the fore of new modes of regulation and accumulation. The compulsion to accumulate overcomes environmental forms that exist within the capitalist mode of production. Capitalism is a contradictory process that results in, what Lipscomb calls the "strengthening of domination and marginalization of counterstruggles that occur."[427] It is not just the control over Nature but the "mastery of secondary effects" (*Herrschaft der Nebenfolgen*). Nature cannot be fully subsumed, because it possesses its own logic. Though total domination has not been achieved, the subsumption of Nature under capitalism continues. Moreover, the rhetoric of catastrophe that serves as both a rational and quasi-religious conviction is at work within ecology. As Badiou reminds us, it is the work of philosophy to reconstruct the contradictions and struggles among societal relationships with Nature and pose a radical way out of the impasse that preserves reason, argumentation and the invention of a new modern tradition, maintaining equality as its ideal.

For Marcuse, the traditional dialectic between humanity and Nature was surpassed in late industrial capitalism when technology replaced Nature as the dominant other and achieved an ideological status. Marcuse argues that political change requires the need to oppress the master of technology in order to gain freedom and re-establish harmony with Nature. Whereas humans were subservient to Nature in the pre-industrial period, technology became a liberator, achieving the status of the oppressor. Technology takes Nature's place as locating human existence in the world and in history. Marcuse argues that this process was not a choice but a historical consequence.[428] The relation between humans, technology, and Nature inherently contains the idea that contemporary living is a form of artificial life. The good life offered by technology is putatively better than before, and, in its essence, militates against qualitative change. As such, the conflict between essence and appearing becomes expendable, if not meaningless. In the process, technology becomes ideology for Marcuse, with capitalism's quantification of all as commodity, leading ineluctably to:

> the quantification of nature, which led to its explication in terms of mathematical structures, separated reality from all inherent ends and, consequently, separated the true from the good, science from ethics…If the Good and the Beautiful, Peace and Justice cannot be derived either from ontological or scientific-rational conditions, they cannot logically claim universal validity and realization…[In a world where science is the only adjudicator of truth] the ideas [of The Good, Beautiful, Peace, Justice] become more ideals, and their concrete, critical content evaporates into the ethical or metaphysical atmosphere.[429]

Under the laws of capital and the state, truth is then confined to a one-dimensional world of facts. Conquering Nature, then, remains the main social priority of humankind. The replacement of Nature by technology changes the relationship of these societies not only to Nature and to technology, but also to themselves and to their self-understanding, where technological rationality is part of a series of reality principles and there exists no outside from the infallibility of the desiring human machine.

Deep ecology shares with the Frankfurt School the idea that the planet is not moving in the direction of progress but catastrophe. It proposes the protection of species in order to save the world from eco-system collapse, partially by reducing the human population. Yet its attachment to uncritical militancy (i.e. support for targeted assassinations of humans), deep ecology becomes an unwitting accomplice to the forces it seeks to overcome, fixated as it is on sacrificial desire. Deep ecology articulates a relationship to wildness being presented as a sacred duty, as a call from The Great Spirit. In confronting the logic of sacrifice, there is a need to overcome the disease of a kind of green nihilism.

Adorno tells us there is an alternative to sacrifice, like in Badiou, where we move from *courage* to *fearlessness* through the subject who maintains fidelity to the event. In deep ecology, then, is a deification of Nature that is a closure to *thinking* climate change. Like Adorno's critique of identitarian thinking, the spirit is sacrificed to rational calculation. Instrumental reason is the *means* and *material for* domination.[430] Ecological living ought to be distinguished from *dwelling,* but is closer to the anticipation of the *not yet.*[431] There is an absence of recognition between subject and object, of history and Nature. Within these divisions is the opportunity to grasp the contradictory, paradoxical features that propose an interpretive method through the event. In Marx's words, "history can be considered from two sides, divided into the history of nature and the history of mankind. Yet there is no separating the two sides; as long as men exist, natural and human history will qualify each other."[432]

Capitalism, in this analysis, has permeated the psychology and biology of human civilization. According to Adorno,

> The inner constitution of the individual, not merely his social role, could be deduced from this…Only when the process that begins with the metamorphosis of labour-power into a commodity has permeated men through and through and objectified each of their impulses as formally commensurable variations of the exchange relationship, is it possible for life to reproduce itself under the prevailing relations of production.[433]

Heidegger's former student, Hans Jonas, writes of "harmonizing humanity with life of Earth as a whole." He argues that Heidegger's notion of a "standing reserve" *to be used* should be contrasted with Nature as phenomena to be *lived with*.[434] If instrumental reason converts all Nature in to standing reserve, then the relation of Nature to alienation views Nature anthropocentrically, particularly with its move from the natural world to an artificial one structured and reorganized for human purposes. *Ecological Metapolitics* critiques the technological practices that function outside of an understood relation to Nature and is radically motivated by a desire to overcome the idea of thinking anthropocentrically.

Transcending Stupidity and the Logics of Capital Flows

The overturning of the contemporary form of neoliberal capitalism is *sine qua non* to answering the questions posed by the question of ecology today. It involves designing new forms of life and new forms of world making. But the human as master and possessor of Nature, from bio-hacker to geo-engineer, only invents new forms of power, organization, and technology in an attempt to maintain the human mastery over Nature. The search for other worlds through space exploration is a new form of mastery over the world through technology, and may well eventually produce a new *nomos* of the universe, where we can evoke Schmitt's mentioning of the future possibility of *cosmopirates* and *cosmopartisans*.[435] Only through making a change in Nature do we change the world and ourselves, but humans are exceptions among the species who singularly have the capacity to bring about the end of the world for themselves and other living beings. In that sense, for Badiou, the solution to the problem of ecology today is specifically a human problem with only a human solution. So although there is a desire to decenter the human being, humanity remains the primary problem and the mode of adjudication; this is also, however, compounded by the fact that Nature also has its own processes of adjudication, beyond the human.

Technology is one of the primary modes by which the human will to power is reified, expressed, and channeled. And, in these technologically mediated human conceptualizations of reality, is the experience of life that reinforces the disconnection between history and Nature. This knowledge of our collective role in the catastrophe invokes the line from the Bhagavad Gita—*Now I am become Death, destroyer of worlds*—that was quoted by Robert Oppenheimer in relation to the detonation of the atomic bomb. Ecology today is being called to internalize and transcend the critique of the Enlightenment. What is being called forth is the need to reconstruct our world and ourselves, as a cooperative project of a radically just distribution – in the process, to reinvent democracy in the real.

Through fidelity to the event, we must seek to clarify where we have choices and where we do not. Inscribed within this challenge is the question, how do we think the impossible in the era of global capitalism as absolute hegemony? The event proposes a rupture between capitalism and modernity, where the truth, in its appearing, exempts itself from *what there is*. The event is not only an exception, but is singular - it does not simply repeat what was formerly possible. Through the appearing of truth, freedom affirms equality against capitalism, in Badiou's ontology. In ecology, the rational redistribution of the sensible metabolic interaction between humanity and Nature brings into the field of play a radical politics at the global scale. When a simulacrum of the truth appears in the (un)Real of the state, it is the example of the mass horrors of the 20th century. Badiou argues that the *real* functions as the main form of thinking the impossible, opening up the space of emancipatory politics. Revolution is, ultimately, a rupture with the finitude of the limited political horizon policed by state and capital; it is a joyous event that transforms subjectivity. It asks, what is the ideal of existence: a good life or a true life? And it asks one to make a choice between the peace of the world as it is, or something like a fidelity to the rupture of what exists towards the *becoming* of the impossible. The event is not the possibility of something new; it is the wager of *the possibility of the possibility of something new* put to chance.[436]

Philosophy's task is, therefore, a call for untimeliness and transgression. It is to break through the nexus between state and capital formations and their definition of the horizon of political possibility. Beyond the Leviathan is true political possibility as a consequence of the event. Philosophy has the task to affirm a project in which, to quote Fanon, "decolonization transforms spectators crushed with their inessentiality into privileged actors, with the grandiose glare of history's floodlights upon them."[437] This is not unlike the subject in relation to the event. Ecology *can be thought* by understanding the event, which can in turn create a subject and a sequence that reworks the relation between humanity and Nature with, in Badiou's words, the possibility of *revolution, passion, invention, and creation,* and beyond the limitations imposed upon political possibility by the structures of state and capital. Only by taking a subtractive distance from the state and capital can the new political possibility of ecology be thought. This is the project of *Ecological Metapolitics*—to think the sequence of ecological change as thought for the generic, the multiplicity, and the infinite while understanding the irreducibility of the human subject as such.

Weather-Making, Artificial Life and the Nomos of the Air

"Revolution makes for beautiful weather."[438]

When Guy Debord wrote this in 1971, he could not have imagined what was on the horizon of possibility. Today, technology is such that human beings have the capacity to actually manipulate the weather. We are living in the extremes of artificial life. Ours is an extreme mastery over Nature that is imprecise and unpredictable, but the possibilities are only now just beginning to show their true face. Within the absurdity of the coming paradox is determining where and what is the *impossible change* that can be made possible. In *Terror from the Air*, Peter Sloterdijk coined the term *airquake* and defined it as an instance in which, the explication of air, climatic and atmospheric situations calls into question the basic presumption of beings concerning their primary media of existence and convicts it of naivety…they enjoyed a privilege of naivety which was withdrawn with the caesura of the 20th century.[439]

In the 1996 U.S. Department of Defense paper, "Weather as a Force Multiplier: Owning the Weather in 2025," a case is made for battlefield shaping of the air and weather as a part of strategic military planning:

A high-risk, high reward endeavor, weather modification offers a dilemma not unlike the splitting of the atom. While some segments of society will always be reluctant to examine controversial issues such as weather modification, the tremendous military capabilities that could result from this field are ignored at our own peril.[440]

When Joseph Conrad wrote in *Heart of Darkness* that, "the conquest of the earth…is not a pretty thing when you look into it too much," he was speaking of the land and the sea, of capitalism and colonialism.[441] The air, the weather, and the cosmos of outer space is a new terrain of struggle and brings new philosophical questions into the field of consideration. What would have been deemed the subject matter of conspiracy theories a few decades ago now comprises the serious research projects of geo-engineering, drone warfare, robot armies, and satellite manipulation. Many on the North American right wing do not believe that global warming is real. For the right wing that *does* recognize the existence of climate change, however, regulating capitalism is not within the realm of ideological possibility. This latter group support geo-engineering on the basis that American ingenuity and innovation with military level intervention protects the repetition of contemporary capitalism as such. They argue that since humans have been sending all kinds of materials into the atmosphere, geo-engineering proposes a realistic stop-gap measure as an interim gesture. Geopolitical analysts have made an industry out of perceived threats to the domestic and global order. In the UK, *Lifeboat Britain* is the term used for the argument to build barriers and deal with climate refugees with protective domestic measures.[442] Other security analysts forecast asymmetrical interventions depending on the economic and military power of states:

Nations with the resources to do so may build virtual fortresses around their countries, preserving resources for themselves…As famine, disease, and weather-related disasters strike due to the abrupt climate change, many countries' needs will exceed their carrying capacity. This will create a sense of desperation, which is likely to lead to offensive aggression in order to reclaim balance…Europe will be struggling internally, large numbers of refugees washing up on its shores and Asia in serious crisis over food and water. Disruption and conflict will be endemic features of life. Once again, warfare would define human life. [443]

Central to this line of thought is the idea of moving beyond the system of Western-oriented international law and order created by the Treaty of Westphalia from 1648. Instead, global warming proposes a reconfiguration of the geopolitics of tomorrow that will open up a more volatile, heated terrain that threatens to disrupt the neo-Westphalian regulatory structures of the past centuries. As one military theorist speculates:

The cycle now may be shifting away from stability toward chaos, suggesting that the nation-state may be entering a period in which its usefulness as a concept for organizing societies will be severely challenged…We may expect increasing chaos during the shift from what has been called the 'modern era' to its successor. [444]

With technological innovation and military-style state responses to the problems opened up by the question of ecology, there comes the global warming-fix through rational, technological means accelerated by the crisis. In some sense, it says that the world can go on *as it is* and that technology can solve the crisis, a crisis that results largely from the capitalist distortion of the metabolic interaction between humanity and Nature.

In 1991, when Mt. Pinatubo erupted on Luzon, a Phillipine Island, it sent an aerosol cloud of sulphur dioxide in to the atmosphere that reflected the sun's rays back to the sky, resulting in ten percent of sunlight not reaching the earth's surface. [445] David Keith, an engineering professor, has argued, "…when you start to reflect light away from the planet, you can easily imagine a chain of events that would extinguish life on the planet." [446] Nature has a way of regulating itself beyond any notion of the human species that has sought, and continues to seek, its mastery. There are inherent risks in attempting geo-engineering and there are risks in not attempting it. There is a false state and capitalist logic of the limitation of choices being presented that reflects a closure of thinking at the level of systems change. What is being proposed through geo-engineering as the solution to global warming is the continuation of the capitalist world as it is.

Scientists today predict, at the modest end of the scale, temperature rises between 1.1 and 2.9 degrees Celsius by the end of this century. More pessimistic predictions set the change between 2.4 to 6.4 degrees Celsius. The melting of the Arctic permafrost would release massive amounts of CO_2 and methane into the atmosphere, to take just one example of the many feedback loops that would be initiated, including warming oceans. While reducing the pace of global warming might be possible through geo-engineering, it will not effect the acidification of oceans that is already underway. Other speculative interventions include mixing the oceans technologically to create a giant foamy bubble bath that would reflect sunlight back in to the sky.[447]

If developed industrial nations embark on this ethically dubious intervention at a grand scale, that then result in drought or impacts on farming of developing nations, what mode of adjudication is possible? On what basis could it be considered legitimate? As one scientist argues:

> People get themselves balled up into knots whether this can be done unilaterally or by one group or one nation. Well, guess what. We decide to do much worse than this every day, and we decide unilaterally. We are polluting the earth unilaterally. Whether it's life-taking decisions, like wars, or something like a trade embargo, the world is about people taking action, not agreeing to take action. And, frankly, the Maldives could say, 'Fuck you all—we want to stay alive.' Would you blame them? Wouldn't any reasonable country do the same?[448]

Yet some would argue that there is a need to move beyond a naïve view of Nature—that, in fact, Nature already is "violent, amoral, and nihilistic."[449] Geo-engineering, as one type of intervention, can be defined as the "deliberate large-scale manipulation of the planetary environment to counteract anthropogenic climate change."[450] One such project argues for sulfates being released into the atmosphere to reduce incoming solar radiation. Part of the argument claims that since humans already emit all sorts of materials into the atmosphere, there is really no moral quandary in releasing other materials that can somehow slow down the effects of global warming, albeit temporarily. If it is possible, should we not try? But how is it decided and who decides? Ultimately, new questions of sovereignty and the need for a new *nomos* of the earth come to the surface through the problems opened up by ecology.

How can climate modification be authorized in the order of things, within the *nomos of the earth*, as an intervention and in whose name? What is the meaning of sovereignty beyond the nation-state in the future when we take the Great Game to the air? Will this simply carry on the repetition with *what already is*. Is it just an extension of the mastery of the Nature from the Enlightenment tradition whether we decide to change the weather or explore the possibilities of space exploration to look for *another place to live?* Does it require a kind of mutation of values? For some, this is an opportunity to overcome the appeals of moral emergency that surround discussions around global warming, but still reinforces the idea that human beings are self-governing and fundamentally apart from Nature. In framing these ideas around an emergency, it can obscure what is actually at stake, for it creates the opening for the state of exception. By intervening in this way, philosopher Stephen Gardiner argues that geo-engineering, "arbitrarily marginalizes central moral issues such as how we get into this predicament and why we are not seriously pursuing better ways out."[451]

Geo-engineering is an intervention that involves the relationship of humanity to the rest of the world, and the movement from the present to the future. It is a reactive response to an emergency put into motion by an existential collective threat. In its name, what follows is the potential adjudication either by the state of such an intervention or its double, a kind of anarchist ecological cowboy intervention, a geo-hacking "solution" to ecological problems albeit at a smaller scale (e.g., iron dumping from ships in to the ocean without legal authority).[452] If one intervenes with geo-engineering methods for the hypothetical good of addressing global warming, such technology can be weaponized against rivals. Geo-engineering potentially opens up a new game of economic terror through geopolitical weather engineering. This type of militarized geo-engineering is within the capacity and reach of some of the larger nation-states and could open up new problems under the name of ecology and other moral claims.

The effects of this possible intervention are both global and intergenerational. Every living being will be impacted, including those who do not yet exist, as future weather patterns will be disrupted by the interventions of today. What are the consequences for human existence if we begin large-scale transformations of the earth's climate? CO_2 persists in the atmosphere for centuries, with impacts certain to be felt by future generations. Geo-engineering potentially represents a transformation of the earth's atmosphere that will exist beyond a human life span—beyond the moment when a choice is made to intervene, leading us to the question, is it possible to make an ethical distinction between natural harms and anthropogenic harms? Since it is human intervention that accelerates and creates the change in weather patterns and warming, what is the harm in experimenting and prototyping scientific interventions that, if tested, could prove to be beneficial? For Badiou, ethics are not universalizable, they are situation-specific and do not involve mediation by the state. Any discussion of environmental ethics even on these new problems fails to meet the standard of truth as part of a materialist dialectics proposed by Badiou.

Within ecology is the idea that there are limits to the human ability to control Nature and that a new vision of modernity is possible beyond the limits of the state and capitalist subjectivity. As we already know, global warming threatens to destroy entire species and ecosystems, and to contribute to the continued acidification of the oceans. The earth, on the one hand, operates according to its own laws and natural processes, but is not apart from human life. There is also resistance from the earth itself to submit to human mastery. It could be argued that late capitalism also transforms the earth's atmosphere in innumerable ways, so why is there not the same ethical concern as there is with geo-engineering? Geo-engineering would be just one more way that humanity manipulates their relation to Nature, so why is this one intervention, geo-engineering, considered an ethical question while everything else we collectively send into the atmosphere is considered beyond ethics, a kind of business as usual?

For conservatives who do believe in climate change, geo-engineering offers an intervention that does not involve greater regulation of the private sector's extractive industries, and that thereby allows for expansion of military interventions and investment in technologies. This follows the Enlightenment tradition that a rational subject displays mastery over a passive Nature combined with the dialectical reluctance of the earth to submit to this mastery in spite of the zeitgeist of technological hubris, once again viewing the Earth as an object in-itself. With these possible interventions, global warming would still cause acidification of the oceans; and the melting of the polar ice could still alter the rotation speed of the earth and its orientation in the solar system.

Geo-engineering proposes that we make a wager to save the world because it is the only world we have. Yet we must challenge not just our understanding of the world but ourselves as moral subjects. Geo-engineering, as such, must also be seen as an act of despair or melancholy—a cynical gesture that denies root causes. Capitalism has created conditions that are comprehensible, but remain destructive – and, more fundamentally, conceal that destruction at a planetary scale. The human population has increased from 800 million in 1750 to 7 billion in 2010,[453] and this expansion is so far beyond any other measurable change in human history that a reckoning is in order according to climate scientists. When evaluating solutions to the problem of ecology, the question becomes what is worth risking, and do we have a mandate to take certain risks? However, as of yet, there is no new *nomos* of the earth capable of adjudicating responses to the scale of change being presented by the Anthropocene.[454]

In this sense, geo-engineering presented as solution, is a posed from inside the subjectivity of the state, as part of a global ordering of state-level responses to global warming. As intervention, it does not adequately present an outside. It asks us to accept the world *as it is*, in order to save us from ourselves. To do this, we must accept the laws of the world, inequality, capitalism and so on, while the geo-engineering fix is administered by particular interests and particular states of the world, who happen to have a technologically developed status. Although a minority within their own movement, those pillars of the American right who acknowledge the phenomenon of global warming (such as Newt Gingrich) argue that "geoengineering holds forth the promise of address-ing global warming concerns for just a few billion dollars a year. Instead of penalizing ordinary Americans, we would have an option to address global warming by rewarding scientific invention…Bring on the Ameri-can ingenuity."[455] In tampering with global temperature, someone inevita-bly gets screwed as the effects of geo-engineering are asymmetrical – the poorest inevitably suffer the greatest consequences. As Latour writes, the true lesson of Frankenstein is that we must learn to love our monsters.[456]

In 2008, during the Beijing Olympics, the Chinese military fired 1,000 rockets in to the atmosphere to attempt to prevent rain.[457] Those who support the idea of human mastery over the climate in the form of solar radiation management subscribe to a mechanical conception of Nature. Plans to geo-engineer the earth fall in line with the objectification of Nature for human needs and take the *techne* of artificial life to new di-mensions. The sovereignty and flatness of land, coupled with its systems of control and bracketing, is taken to the air as part of a new *nomos* of the earth, in a reactionary attempt to overcome resistance to the idea that hu-mans can master Nature. We know we are destroying the earth in a way that has infinite existential and material consequence for human beings and other species. Even if global warming would be more dramatic than the side effects of a technological intervention, geo-engineering poses a solution to a problem without asking the right question. Geo-engineering, in other words, involves a de-linking of climate change and justice. As Clive Hamilton has written:

> So we can see that, far from being a phenomenon limited to changes in the weather, human-induced climate change is bringing everything into play in ways that appear increasingly complex and beyond control. Yet plans for solar radiation management challenge the earth as a whole to present itself to us as a system that can be understood, manipulated, and regulated. These facts call not for more calculation of risks but for a radical change in the modern conception of the earth and a repudiation of the idea of the modern subject that founds climate ethics. It is a call for a new kind of subject, the heteronomous subject who recognizes sources of moral authority beyond human calculation in the understanding of the world suggested to us by earth-system science.[458]

Geo-engineering, for others, is mere *planet hacking* carrying out design thinking on a grand scale scrambling "old political alliances and carv[ing] out new ideological fault lines."[459] In this sense, there could be some legitimate claims to the idea that *whose hand is on the global thermostat is the hand that rules the world.* For those who support the continued human mastery over Nature, apocalyptic scenarios would be dethroned by technological solutions. Keeping the world as it is, in its ideological desire for an unequal order, will require the construction of new narrative arcs, new lies, and new transgressions by state and capital to retain the maximal limit points of sovereign power. Built into the proposition of geo-engineering is the fear of trans-boundary harm, the willful betrayal of the scientific precautionary principle, and symptomatic of an alienated relation to intergenerational equity. All the while, we remain with an unanswered question, *what is my relation to those not yet living?* As Sloterdijk writes, "So long as meteorology presents itself as a natural science and nothing else, it can pass in silence over the question of the weather's possible author." [460]

Ecological Metapolitics proposes a rupture to the repetition of the world *as it is*; transcending the imagination and capability of contemporary ethical demands that have their basis within the incumbent culture of democratic materialism. Ethical screens, especially ones that perform the policing functions of the acceptable discourse and movement of democratic materialism, are, in reality, ideological ones and in a material way keep things as they are. Geo-engineering doubles down on the capitalist world *as it is* by affirming a trajectory for collective living that reinforces inequality. It is a simulacrum of an event.

What is the Time of This Time?

The desire to control Nature is linked to outdated modes of contemporary and future survival, resulting in the continued human domination over Nature. This modality raises the question of what historical time does *Ecological Metapolitics* inhabit, or as Michael Lipscomb writes, regarding climate change, "what is the time of this time, or the tempo, of this historical moment and its unfolding"?[461] It entails, following Walter Benjamin, an elaboration of *now time*. For Benjamin Bratton, the problem of ecology results in a disoriented, dialectical relation between present and future, writing that:

> instead of locating the post-Anthropocene *after* the Anthropocene along some dialectical timeline, it is better conceived as *a composite parasite nested inside the host of present time*, evolving and appearing in irregular intervals at a scale that exceeds the *Eros/Thanatos* economy of the organism.[462]

Today, the question of ecology is often linked to the belief that human consumption has overtaken carrying capacity and that we are already in the time of disaster and already at the end of the world, as Morton claims. Given the exigency with which ecology is unfolding, Badiou would argue that Adorno's commitment to democracy might be too slow and muddled a response to Nature today, where there is a tension between anxiety and courage, between the need for urgency and the competing desire for democracy, deliberation and patience. As Lipscomb observes, "within the totalizing tendencies of an age that colonizes our bodies and our minds, the question of what constitutes a proper counter-signature becomes a matter of central importance."[463]

Patricia Reed writes that our relation to geological time requires a need to:

acknowledge a radical asymmetry of temporal scaling that calls for mediation. Grand scales of time resist our phenomenological grasp (we can never experience millions of years, or the preconscious universe), yet if humans are to have a chance in the post-anthropocene, we need cognitive and affective openings to be perceptually engineered. Assuming a spacetime dynamism, unlike the static capture of objects in linear perspective, this new perspectival orientation must adopt a geometry that augments our phenomenological constraints; a nested spacetime complexity that could render that which, in the linear-visual world, vanishes at the illusion of a horizon.[464]

Humans, either as subjects or objects in the Anthropocene, are dealing with a disoriented relation to time. Inscribed within *Ecological Metapolitics* is a desire to open up the political imaginary to *infinite interruptions to the way things are* as an opening for the inscription of a countersignature—the possibility of the possibility of something new. Time may be a problem of the political future, but the composition of the present is what remains at stake as a political question today. Badiou writes, "to live is thus an incorporation into the present under the faithful form of a subject."[465] There is a dissonance between the need to act now in order to protect the future of the collective and to live now and let technological determinism solve the problem of the future. It is this ringing of the alarm bell, of a call that is urgently made, and in whose name the shadows of monsters appear that ultimately transforms the situation in to a disaster in the waiting.[466] For Badiou, history is a construction in the present that serves particular interests, going even so far in *Theory of the Subject* as to state that "history does not exist."[467]

Within ecology, generational debts are projected onto an imaginary future and moral claims to do what is right in the present violently conflict with capitalist culture's mode of operation—i.e. with the development of contemporary desire, the perpetual pursuit of instant gratification. Within this dilemma is the question, *I just have this life to live, what should I do with it?* For Serres, because the earth is being transformed by our doing, it has a subject once again. He writes, "this crisis of foundations is not an intellectual crisis; it does not affect our ideas or language or logic or geometry, but time and weather and our survival." [468]

Badiou, following Lacan, says "do not give up on your desire."
He argues that we must live the true life in support of the Idea. Within
the symptomatic torsion of its limit point is the metabolic *field of play*
between humanity and Nature. To work around it, or to move through
the problem of ecology, however, we will need a reawakening. We may
not need something new, but we may need to bring back to life something dormant today, which is a reinvention of something familiar. That
reinvention is a desire for a *new modern tradition*—a non-capitalist
modernity—a repetition on the side of the continuation of Nature that
acknowledges its living interaction with humanity and other living beings
in the world, while acknowledging the singularity of the human capacity
to destroy life on earth. Inscribed within *Ecological Metapolitics*, is an
attempt to listen closely to this notion of political change and to subtract
oneself from the structure of what has traditionally been referred to as
'environmental philosophy' – a field that represents a closure to thinking
change regarding the question of ecology today. *Ecological Metapolitics*
is an intervention to identify what is different than what came before
regarding the politics of ecology, and to locate change in the movement
from the present to the future that has equality as its basis.

In the arrhythmic variations and dialectical movements of global
systems, we remain imprisoned in narrow, localized earthly domains.
Amidst the immediate reckonings of these localized orbits, we may have
already lost the world. Nature is exacting revenge as a form of justice as
a substitute for other means of adjudication, for they do not yet exist in
adequate form. It is the task of philosophy to determine what are the new
questions to be asked today. In order to truly live in this world, for Badiou, there is a call for a fundamental transformation and a new orientation
to discover the true life, and existence as such, through fidelity to the
event. It remains the task of philosophy to not accept the world as it is, to
construct the outlines of a new, impossible world - it is a desire to invent
something fundamentally new. For Badiou, philosophy is ultimately
axiom-based. Let us end then, with these axioms as our countersignature
for *Ecological Metapolitics* today:

Philosophy must speak in its own name as a poetic articulation of the true life.

The hypothesis for an ecological vision today requires a new subject and a non-capitalist modernity.

The desire for revolution is ultimately a desire for justice.

We are nothing, let us be everything.

The World needs a new kind of Love that is part of a new modern tradition. A Love beyond Nature that is a Universe - a Love of the Infinite that is the Secret Truth of the World for All.

CONCLUSION

To think through ecology philosophically, it is vital to use the conditions of politics, love, science and art, that Badiou proposes as the truth conditions of philosophy in order to avert the disaster of suturing philosophy to politics. *Ecological Metapolitics* is defined as, the consequences a philosophy is capable of drawing from the real instances of the political project of ecology as thought. *Ecological Metapolitics* proposes for philosophy an ontology that thinks the possibilities of ecological political change from the perspective of the subject, for the preservation of the future of the natural world and living beings in our own time, and in to the future. In thinking through the problem of ecology and the Anthropocene, a new relation is posited to the present, to the future and serves as a new meditation on death.

Ecological Metapolitics represents a new relationship between humanity and science. It is a forceful attempt to continue the existence of the collective as such, constituted within the world of change that places humanity as a part of Nature, not apart from it. It recognizes the singularity of the human species in its capacity to destroy the world of living beings on the earth and for the capacity of Nature to destroy humanity and the worlds of living things.

Philosophy should create, but not with negation as its first move. Philosophy is an affirmative construction concerned with the production of new truths in our own time. Philosophy's task is to prepare for the event by encouraging the movement of the impossible in to the realm of the possible. In ecology, there is a contradiction between the state of affairs and being. When the subject is seized by an event, it changes something of the real in their subjective determination.

149

What is called for today is a rupture between capitalism and modernity in opposition to the abolition of future being presented as the law of finitude. A non-capitalist modernity is a world that ecology proposes today. From the specifics of its localization, it must propose a universality that everyone can participate in the name of equality in order to overcome the amnesia and denial embedded in the question of ecology today. The political invention of truth is an act of division, constructed at a distance from the state and capital, rather than an act of consensus, involving a seizure of truths. Moving from the one to the infinite, from the specific to the universal, is how philosophy thinks politics according to Badiou.

Ecological Metapolitics is a means of thinking the politics of ecology, through the subject of the event, as thought. The problem of ecology today presupposes a change that involves resistance to the repetition of the world *as it is* by a subject that has fidelity to an event. Only as a consequence of the event will the subject come in to being. Inside the question of ecology is the fear of the consequences of the *passion for the real* that is a lasting legacy of the last century. Resulting from the call for emergency, the problem of ecology and the possibility of new technological interventions, is the emergence of new sovereign forms that will be stacked upon old models – inevitably, this will raise new questions of sovereignty, open up new fragmentations and friend-enemy distinctions. Within these movements, from the local to the global, and back again, is the irreducible subject as such, a new ecological partisan, as a consequence of, and in fidelity to, the event.

BIBLIOGRAPHY

Adorno, Theodor W. *The Culture Industry: Selected Essays on Mass Culture.*
New York: Routledge, 2001.

_____. W. with Horkheimer, Max. *Dialectic of Enlightenment.* trans. Edmund
Jephcott. Stanford: Stanford University Press, 2002.

_____. . *Negative Dialectics.* trans. E.B. Ashton. London: Continuum Books,
2007.

Agamben, Giorgio. *Homo Sacer: Sovereign Power and Bare Life.* trans. Daniel
Heller-Roazen. Stanford: Stanford University Press, 1998.

_____. . *Means Without End: Notes on Politics.* trans. Vincenzo Binetti and Ce-
sare Casarino. Minneapolis: University of Minnesota Press, 2000.

_____. . *State of Exception,* trans. Kevin Attell, Chicago: University of Chicago
Press, 2005.

Agamben, Giorgio. *What Is an Apparatus? and other essays.* Stanford: Stanford
University Press, 2009.

Badiou, Alain. *Affirmative Dialectics: from Logic to Anthropology.* International
Journal of Badiou Studies, Volume Two Number ONE.

_____. *Being and Event.* trans. Oliver Feltham. London: Continuum Books,
2005.

_____. *The Adventure of French Philosophy.* trans. Bruno Bosteels. London:
Verso Books, 2012.

_____. *The Century.* trans. Alberto Toscano. Cambridge: Polity Press, 2007.

_____. *The Communist Hypothesis,* trans. by David Macey and Steve Corcoran.
London: Verso Books, 2010.

_____. *Conditions,* trans. Steve Corcoran. London: Continuum Books, 2008.

_____. *Ethics: An Essay on the Understanding of Evil.* trans. Peter Hallward.
London: Verso Books, 2001.

_____. *Infinite Thought: Truth and Return to Philosophy,* trans. and ed. by Oliver
Feltham and Justin Clemens. London: Continuum Books, 2003.

Badiou, Alain and Roudinesco, Elisabeth. *Jacques Lacan: Past and Present: A
Dialogue.* trans. Jason E. Smith. New York: Columbia University Press,
2014.

_____. *Logics of Worlds.* trans. Alberto Toscano. London: Continuum Books,
2009.

_____. *Manifesto for Philosophy.* trans. Norman Madarasz. Albany: SUNY Press, 1999.

_____. *Metapolitics.* trans. Jason Barker. London: Verso, 2005.

_____ (with Tarby, Fabian). *Philosophy and the Event.* trans. Louise Burchill. Cambridge: Polity Press, 2013.

_____. *Philosophy for Militants.* trans. Bruno Bosteels. London: Verso, 2012.

_____. and Zizek, Slavoj. *Philosophy in the Present.* London: Polity Press, 2009.

_____. *Plato's Republic.* trans. Susan Spitzer. New York: Columbia University Press, 2012.

_____. *Polemics,* trans. Steve Corcoran, London: Verso, 2006.

_____. *The Rebirth of History.* trans. Gregory Elliot. London: Verso Books, 2012.

_____. *St. Paul: The Foundation of Universalism.* trans. Ray Brassier. Stanford: Stanford University Press, 2003.

_____. *Second Manifesto for Philosophy.* trans. Louise Burchill. Cambridge: Polity Press, 2011.

_____. *The Subject of Change: Lessons from the European Graduate School,* trans. Duane Rousselle. New York: Atropos Press, 2013.

Barker, Jason. *Alain Badiou: A Critical Introduction.* London: Pluto Press, 2002.

Benjamin, Walter. *On the Concept of History.* trans. Dennis Redmond, Gesammelten Schriften I:2, Suhrkamp Verlag. Frankfurt am Main, 1974.

_____. *Illuminations: Essays and Reflections.* ed. Hannah Arendt, New York: Harcourt Brace Jovanovich, 1968.

Berardi, Franco Bifo. *Accelerationism Questioned from the Point of View of the Body.* e-flux journal #46, June 2013. URL?

Bosteels, Bruno. *Alain Badiou: Key Concepts.* eds. A.J. Bartlett and Jason Clemens. Durham: Acumen Publishing, 2010.

_____. *Badiou and Politics.* Durham: Duke University Press, 2011.

Bratton, Benjamin. *The Black Stack.* e-flux journal #53, March 2014. URL

_____. *On the Nomos of the Cloud.* (2012), http://bratton.info/projects/talks/on-the-nomos-of-the-cloud-the-stack-deep-address-integral-geography/

_____. *Some Trace Effects of the Post-Anthropocene: On Accelerationist Geopolitical Aesthetics.* e-flux journal #46. URL

Brzezinski, Zbigniew. *Between Two Ages: America's Role in the Technetronic Era.* New York: Viking Press, 1970.

_____. *The Choice: Global Domination or Global Leadership.* New York: Basic Books, 2004.

_____. *The Grand Chessboard.* New York: Basic Books, 1997.

Burn, Wil C. G. and Strauss, Andrew L. *Climate Change Geoengineering: Philosophical Perspectives, Legal Issues and Governance Frameworks.* Cambridge: Cambridge University Press, 2013.

Butler, Judith. *Precarious Life: The Powers of Mourning and Violence.* London: Verso, 2004.

Camus, Albert. *The Myth of Sisyphus.* trans. Justin O'Brien. London: Penguin Books, 2006.

Caygill, Howard. *On Resistance: A Philosophy of Defiance.* London: Bloomsbury, 2013.

Celli, Carlo. *Gillo Pontecorvo: From Resistance to Terrorism.* Oxford: The Rowman and Littlefield Publishing Group, 2005.

Conrad, Joseph. *Heart of Darkness.* London: Dover Thrift Editions, 1990.

Coulthard, Glen Sean. *Red Skin, White Masks: Rejecting the Colonial Politics of Recognition.* Minneapolis: University of Minnesota Press, 2014.

_____. "Subjects of Empire: Indigenous Peoples and the 'Politics of Recognition' in Canada," *Contemporary Political Theory,* (2007), **6**, 437–460.

Debord, Guy. *The Sick Planet.* 1971, Published post-humously by Gallimard, in 2004. Translated from the French by NOT BORED! March 2006. It can be accessed here: http://www.notbored.org/the-sick-planet.html

Derrida, Jacques. *The Politics of Friendship.* trans. George Collins, London: Verso, 1994.

_____. *The Work of Mourning.* trans. and ed. Pascale-Anne Brault and Michael Nass. Chicago: University of Chicago Press, 2001.

Engels, Friedrich. 'Outlines of a Critique of Political Economy,' in *Karl Marx: The Economic and Philosophic Manuscripts of 1844.* Ed. Howard Parsons, Marx and Engels on Ecology. Westport, Conn: Greenwood Press, 1977.

Feltham, Oliver. *Alain Badiou: Live Theory.* London: Continuum, 2008.

Fanon, Frantz. *Black Skin White Masks.* trans. Charles Lam Markmann, New York: Grove Press, 1967.

_____. *Wretched of the Earth.* trans. Constance Farrington, New York: Grove Press, 1963.

Feenberg, Andrew. *Heidegger and Marcuse: The Catastrophe and Redemption of History.* New York: Routledge, 2005.

Foster, John Bellamy, Clark, Brett and York, Richard. *The Ecological Rift: Capitalism's War on Earth.* New York: Monthly Review Press, 2010.

_____. *Marx's Ecology: Materialism and Nature.* New York: Monthly Review Press, 2000.

Foucault, Michel. *The Care of the Self: Vol. 3 of the History of Sexuality.* trans. Robert Hurley. New York: Random House Books, 1986.

_____. *The Courage of Truth: The Government of Self and Others II, Lectures at the College de France, 1983-84.* ed. Graham Burchell. New York: Palgrave MacMillan, 2008.

_____. *The Hermeneutics of the Subject: Lectures at the College de France, 1981-82,* trans. Graham Burchell, New York: Picador, 2001.

_____. *History of Sexuality, Vol 1: An Introduction.* New York: Random House, 1978.

_____. *Lectures on The Will to Know: Lectures at the College de France, 1970-71,* trans. Graham Burchell. London: Palgrave MacMillan, 2011.

_____. *Security, Territory, Population 1977-78.* trans. Graham Burchell. New York: Picador, 2007.

_____. *Society Must Be Defended: Lectures at the College de France 1975-76.* trans. David Macey. New York: Picador, 1997.

Freud, Sigmund. *The Standard Edition of the Complete Psychological Works of Sigmund Freud, Vol. XIV,* ed. J. Strachey. London: Hogarth Press, 1956.

Gramsci, Antonio. *The Antonio Gramsci Reader: Selected Writings 1916-1935.* ed. David Forgacs. London: Larence and Wishart, 1999.

Hallward, Peter. *A Subject to Truth.* Minneapolis: University of Minnesota Press, 2003.

Harvey, David. *Justice, Nature and the Geography of Difference.* Oxford: Blackwell Publishing, 1996.

Heidegger, Martin. *Being and Time.* trans. John Macquarrie and Edward Robinson. New York: Harper and Row, 1962.

_____. *The Question Concerning Technology.* trans. William Lovitt. New York: Harper and Row, 1977.

_____. *Towards the Definition of Philosophy.* trans. Ted Sadler. London: Continuum, 2000.

_____. *What is Called Thinking?* trans. J. Glenn Gray. New York: Harper and Row, 1968.

Jameson, Frederic. *Notes on the Nomos,* The South Atlantic Quarterly 104:2, Spring 2005, Duke University Press, 199-204.

Klein, Naomi. *This Changes Everything.* Toronto: Alfred A Knopf Canada, 2014.

Kojève, Alexandre. *Introduction to the Reading of Hegel.* trans. James H. Nichols, Jr. Ithaca: Cornell University Press, 1980.

Kolbert, Elizabeth. *The Sixth Extinction: An Unnatural History.* New York: Henry Hold and Company, 2014.

Lacan, Jacques. *The Four Fundamental Concepts of Psychoanalysis: The Seminar of Jacques Lacan Book XI,* ed. Jacques-Alain Miller. trans. Alan Sheridan. New York: W.W. Norton and Company, 1981.

Lefebvre, Henri. *The Production of Space.* trans. Donald Nicholson-Smith. Oxford: Blackwell Publishers, 1974.

Lenin, Vladimir. *One Step Forward, Two Steps Back,* trans. Shameem Faizee. New Delhi: People's Publishing House, 2011.

Mackay, Robin and Avenessian, Armen. eds. #Accelerate#: *The Accelerationist Reader.* Falmouth: Urbanomic, 2014.

Mann, Geoff and Wainwright, Joel. Climate Leviathan. *Antipode* Vol. 00 No. 0

2012 ISSN 0066-4812, pp 1–22.

Marin, Louis and Jameson, Frederic. *Theses on Ideology and Utopia*. Minnesota Review 6.1 (1976): 71-75. Project MUSE.

Marx, Karl. *Grundrisse*. trans. Martin Nicolaus. London: Penguin Books, 1993.

_____. *Karl Marx: Selected Writings*. trans. David MacLellan. Oxford: Oxford University, 2000.

Meillassoux, Quentin. *After Finitude: An Essay on the Necessity of Contingency*, trans. Ray Brassier. London: Continuum Books, 2008.

Moreno, Gene. Editorial. e-flux journal #46, June 2013. URL

Morton, Timothy. Ecology Without Nature: Rethinking Environmental Aesthetics. Cambridge: Harvard University Press, 2007.

_____. Hyperobjects: Philosophy and Ecology After the End of the World. Minneapolis: University of Minnesota, 2013.

Montaigne, Michel de. The Complete Essays of Michel de Montaigne. trans. Charles Cotton. Sioux Falls: NuVision Publications, 2009.

Nietzsche, Friedrich. Ecce Homo. trans. Duncan Large. Oxford: Oxford University Press, 2007.

_____. . Portable Nietzsche. trans. Walter Kaufman. New York: Viking Penguin, 1954.

Parenti, Christian. Tropic of Chaos: Climate Change and the New Geography of Violence. New York: Nation Books, 2011.

Piketty, Thomas. Capital in the Twenty-First Century. trans. Arthur Goldhammer. Cambridge: Harvard University Press, 2014.

Plato. Protagoras and Meno. trans. Adam Beresford. London: Penguin Books, 2005.

Rancière, Jacques. *The Emancipated Spectator,* trans. Gregory Elliot. London: Verso, 2009.

Robinson, Kim Stanley. *Red Mars.* New York: Bantam Books, 1993.

Ronell, Avital. *Stupidity.* Chicago: University of Illinois Press, 2002.

_____. *The Über Reader: Selected Works of Avital Ronell* Chicago: University of Illinois Press, 2008.

Schirmacher, Wolfgang. "Homo Generator: Media and Postmodern Technology. " In *Culture on the Brink: Ideologies of Technology,* eds. Gretchen Bender and Timothy Druckrey, 65-82. Seattle: Bay Press, 1994.

_____. On the World View of a Vita Activa." Original 1985. Translated into English by Ira Allen. It can be accessed here: http://www.egs.edu/faculty/wolfgang-schirmacher/articles/on-the-world-view-of-a-vita-activa/

_____. . "Technoculture and Life Technique," in *Just Living. Philosophy in Artificial Life.* New York: Atropos Press, 2013.

Schmitt, Carl. *Concept of the Political.* trans. George Schwab. Chicago: University of Chicago Press, 1996.

_____. *The Nomos of the Earth.* trans. G.L. Ulmen. New York, Telos Press

Publishing, 2003.

_____. *Political Theology.* trans. George Schwab. Chicago: University of Chicago Press, 1985.

_____. *Theory of the Partisan.* trans. G.L. Ulmen. New York: Telos Press Publishing, 2007.

Serres, Michel. *The Natural Contract.* trans. Elizabeth MacArthur and Williams Paulson. Ann Arbor: University of Michigan, 1995.

Simpson, Leanne. *Dancing on our Turtles Back.* Winnipeg: Arbeiter Ring Publishing, 2011.

Soja, Edward. W. *Postmodern Geographies: The Reassertion of Space in Critical Social Theory.* London: Verso, 2005.

Solnitt, Rebecca. *A Field Guide to Getting Lost.* New York: Viking, 2005.

Sloterdijk, Peter. *Bubbles: Spheres.* trans. Wieland Hoban Cambridge: MIT Press, 2011.

Sloterdijk, Peter and Heinrichs, Hans-Jürgen. *Neither Sun Nor Death.* trans. Steve Corcoran. Los Angeles: Semiotext(e), 2001.

_____. *Rage and Time,* trans. Mario Wenning. New York: Columbia University Press, 2010.

Sloterdijk, Peter. *Terror from the Air.* trans. Amy Patton and Steve Corcoran. Los Angeles: Semiotext(e), 2009.

Smith, Neil. *Uneven Development: Nature, Capital, and the Production of Space.* Athens: University of Georgia Press, 1984.

Sontag, Susan. *Regarding the Pain of Others.* New York: Picador, 2003.

Taussig, Michael. *Shamanism, Colonialism and the Wild Man: A Study in Terror and Healing.* Chicago: University of Chicago Press, 1987.

Vaneigem, Raoul. *The Revolution of Everyday Life.* trans. Donald Nicholson-Smith. London: Rebel Press, 2006.

Weintrobe, Sally. *Engaging with Climate Change: Psychoanalytic and Interdisciplinary Perspectives.* London: Routledge, 2013.

Weizman, Eyal. *Hollow Land: Israel's Architecture of Occupation.* London: Verso, 2007.

Willox, Ashlee Cunsolo. *"The Work of Mourning,"* In *Ethics & The Environment*, Volume 17, Number 2, Fall 2012, 137-164.

Wolin, Richard. *The Heidegger Controversy: Only a God Can Save Us.* Cambridge, MIT Press, 1992.

Richard Wolin, "Introduction to Herbert Marcuse and Martin Heidegger: An Exchange of Letters," *New German Critique* No. 53 (Spring, 1991), pp. 19-27.

Zizek, Slavoj. *Living in the End Times.* London: Verso, 2010.

_____. Philosophy, the "Unknown Knowns," and the Public Use of Reason, *Topoi,* vol. 25, No. 1-2, 2006, 137-42.

Endnotes

1   Alain Badiou, *The Subject of Change: Lessons from the European Graduate School,* trans. Duane Rousselle (New York: Atropos Press, 2013), 5. N.B. Author's Note by Alain Badiou: "This text...reflects an oral contribution, with degree of improvisation, and does not correspond to any text...Consequently any use or quotation of this text will have to be accompanied with a precise indication of its origin, so that nobody could think that I have either written or proof-read it"

2   Ibid., 7.

3   Ibid.

4   Ibid., 2.

5   Ibid., 3.

6   Oliver Feltham, *Alain Badiou: Live Theory* (London: Continuum, 2008), 139.

7   Badiou, *Subject of Change,* 2.

8   Bruno Bosteels, *Alain Badiou: Key Concepts,* ed. A. J. Bartlett and Jason Clemens (Durham: Acumen Publishing, 2010), 143.

9   Badiou, *Subject of Change,* 4.

10   Ibid., 4. An example of conservative change is offered by Marx in the *Eighteenth Brumaire of Louis Bonaparte* in which Bonaparte mobilizes the tradition to foster a repetition against change.

11   Ibid.

12   Michel Serres, *The Natural Contract,* trans. Elizabeth MacArthur and William Paulson (Ann Arbor: University of Michigan Press, 1995), 4.

13   Ibid., 5.

14   Ibid.

15   Ibid., 6.

16   Ibid., 5.

17   Ibid., 6.

18   Ibid.

19   Ibid.

20   Gilles Lipovetsky, "Power of Repetition," *#Accelerate#: The Accelerationist Reader*, eds. Robin Mackay and Armen Avenessian (Falmouth: Urbanomic Media Ltd., 2014), 226-27.

21 Badiou, *Subject of Change*, 7.

22 Alain Badiou, *Plato's Republic*, trans. Susan Spitzer (New York: Columbia UP, 2012), xvii.

23 Badiou, *Subject of Change*, 59.

24 Ibid., 61.

25 Ibid., 6.

26 Ibid.

27 Ibid., 3-4.

28 Ibid., 3.

29 In British Columbia, Canada, for example, investors are currently pitching a $10 billion plan to have the "world's greenest oil refinery."

30 Alain Badiou, *The Communist Hypothesis*, trans. David Macey and Steve Corcoran (London: Verso, 2010), 227.

31 Alain Badiou, *Manifesto for Philosophy*, trans. Norman Madarasz (Albany: SUNY Press, 1999), 58.

32 Ibid.

33 Alain Badiou, "Affirmative Dialectics: from Logic to Anthropology," *International Journal of Badiou Studies* 2.1: 1-4.

34 Badiou, *Subject of Change*, 31.

35 Badiou, "Affirmative Dialectics," 2.

36 Ibid., 3.

37 Ibid.

38 Ibid., 4.

39 Ibid.

40 Wolfgang Schirmacher, "On the World View of a *Vita Activa*" (1985), trans. Ira Allen, *European Graduate School* <http://www.egs.edu/faculty/wolfgang-schirmacher/articles/on-the-world-view-of-a-vita-activa/>.

41 Ibid.

42 Badiou, *Manifesto for Philosophy*, 32.

43 Badiou, *Subject of Change*, 118.

44 Ibid., 118.

45 Badiou, *Key Concepts*, 95.

46 Bruno Bosteels, *Badiou and Politics* (Durham: Duke UP, 2011), 25.

47 Alain Badiou, *The Rebirth of History*, trans. Gregory Elliot (London: Verso, 2012), 63.

48 Alain Badiou, *The Adventure of French Philosophy*, trans. Bruno Bosteels

(London: Verso, 2012), 37.

49   Bosteels, *Badiou and Politics*, 189.

50   Alain Badiou, *The Century*, trans. Alberto Toscano (Cambridge: Polity Press, 2007), 116.

51   Alain Badiou, *Philosophy for Militants*, trans. Bruno Bosteels (London: Verso, 2012), 67.

52   Ibid., 111.

53   Bosteels, *Badiou and Politics*, 193.

54   Ibid., 207.

55   Ibid.

56   Alain Badiou, *Second Manifesto for Philosophy*, trans. Louise Burchill (Cambridge: Polity Press, 2011), 130.

57   Slavoj Žižek, Living *in the End Times* (London: Verso, 2010), 353.

58   Badiou, *Second Manifesto for Philosophy*, 45.

59   Ibid., 105.

60   Alain Badiou, *Logics of Worlds*, trans. Alberto Toscano (London: Continuum, 2009), 510.

61   Thank you to Samir Gandesha for making this connection for me.

62   Ibid., xvi

63   Alain Badiou (with Fabian Tarby), *Philosophy and the Event*, trans. Louise Burchill (Cambridge: Polity Press, 2013), 148.

64   Alain Badiou, *Ethics: An Essay on the Understanding of Evil*, trans. Peter Hallward (London: Verso Books, 2001), xi

65   Ibid., 128.

66   Ibid., 130.

67   Badiou, *Ethics*, 113.

68   Bosteels, *Badiou and Politics*, 168.

69   Ibid., 17.

70   Taken from notes from a master class with Alain Badiou in Amsterdam, March 2012, at the Amsterdam School of Cultural Analysis. Was there a title to the seminar? If so I would avoid "notes" and list the seminar title, place, date, etc.

71   Badiou, *Subject of Change*, 63.

72   Badiou, *Metapolitics*, 145.

73   Taken from notes from a master class with Alain Badiou in Amsterdam, March 2012, at the Amsterdam School of Cultural Analysis.

74   Ibid.

75 Ibid.

76 Jason Barker, *Alain Badiou: A Critical Introduction* (London: Pluto Press, 2002), 131.

77 Ibid, 131.

78 Taken from notes from a master class with Alain Badiou in Amsterdam, March 2012, at the Amsterdam School of Cultural Analysis.

79 Barker, *Alain Badiou: A Critical Introduction,* 59.

80 Badiou, *Subject of Change,* 27.

81 Ibid., 116.

82 Ibid., 8.

83 Ibid., 71.

84 Robin Mackay and Armen Avenessian, *Introduction,* #Accelerate#: The Acclerationist Reader, eds. Robin Mackay and Armen Avanessian, (Falmouth, Urbanomics, 2014),12.

85 Peppe Savá, "'God didn't die, he was transformed into money': An Interview with Giorgio Agamben," *libcom.org* (10 Feb. 2014) <http://libcom.org/library/god-didnt-die-he-was-transformed-money-interview-giorgio-agamben-peppe-savà>.

86 Badiou, *Logics of Worlds,* 509.

87 Roy Scranton, "Learning How to Die in the Anthropocene," *The New York Times* (13 Nov. 2013) <http://opinionator.blogs.nytimes.com/2013/11/10/learning-how-to-die-in-the anthropocene/?_php=true&_type=blogs&_r=0>.

88 Michel de Montaigne, *The Complete Essays of Michel de Montaigne,* trans. Charles Cotton (Sioux Falls: NuVision Publications, 2009), 47.

89 Albert Camus, *The Myth of Sisyphus,* trans. Justin O'Brien (Harmondsworth: Penguin Books, 1975), 11.

90 Badiou, *The Subject of Change: Lessons from the European Graduate School,* 8.

91 Ibid., 9.

92 From notes at a masterclass with Alain Badiou at Amsterdam School of Cultural Analysis, University of Amsterdam, March 2013.

93 Badiou writes, "Lacan's contribution today is as a result fundamentally double: on the one hand, it makes a possible a limpid structural comprehension of the crisis as a symbolic crisis or crisis of the symbolic; on the other hand, he makes possible the affirmation of the irreducibility of the desiring subject as such" in: Alain Badiou and Elisabeth Roudinesco, *Jacques Lacan: Past and Present: A Dialogue,* trans. Jason E. Smith (New York: Columbia UP, 2014), 61.

94 Judith Butler, *Precarious Life: The Powers of Mourning and Violence* (London: Verso, 2004), xx.

95 Ibid., 21.

96 Ibid., xvi.

97 Ashlee Cunsolo Willox, "Climate Change as the Work of Mourning," *Ethics & the Environment* 17.2 (Fall 2012).

98 Ibid.

99 Ibid.

100 Ibid

101 Ibid.

102 Jacques Derrida, *The Work of Mourning,* ed. and trans. Pascale-Anne Brault and Michael Nass, (Chicago: U of Chicago P, 2001), 72.

103 Ibid., 15.

104 Ibid., 16.

105 Willox, "Climate Change as the Work of Mourning," *Ethics & the Environment* 17.2 (Fall 2012).

106 Derrida, *The Work of Mourning,* 107.

107 Seminar with Giorgio Agamben, European Graduate School, August 2013.

108 Žižek, *Living in the End Times,* xi-xii.

109 Timothy Morton, *Ecology Without Nature: Rethinking Environmental Aesthetics* (Cambridge: Harvard UP, 207), 119.

110 Ibid.

111 Nina Power and Alberto Toscano, *Alain Badiou: Key Concepts,* ed. A. J. Bartlett and Jason Clemens (Durham: Acumen Publishing, 2010), 104.

112 Alain Badiou, *Ethics: An Essay on the Understanding of Evil,* trans. Peter Hallward (London: Verso, 2001), 90.

113 Alain Badiou, *Metapolitics,* trans. Jason Barker (London: Verso, 2005), xxxix.

114 Ibid., 10.

115 Ibid.

116 Badiou, *Logics of Worlds,* 511.

117 Ibid., 16.

118 Ibid., 23.

119 Ibid.

120 Ibid., 24.

121 Ibid., xi.

122 Ibid., xi-xii.

123 Alain Badiou, *The Communist Hypothesis,* trans. David Macey and Steve Corcoran (London: Verso, 2010), 155.

124 Badiou, *Metapolitics,* vii.

125 Badiou, *Metapolitics,* 145.

126 Barker, *Alain Badiou: A Critical Introduction,* 4.

127 Ibid., 58.

128 Ibid., 94.

129 Ibid., 134.

130 Ibid., 135.

131 Alain Badiou, *Manifesto for Philosophy,* trans. Norman Madarasz (Albany: SUNY Press, 1999), 113.

132 Barker, *Alain Badiou: A Critical Introduction,* 115.

133 Alain Badiou, *Infinite Thought: Truth and the Return to Philosophy,* trans. and ed. by Oliver Feltham and Justin Clemens (London: Continuum, 2003), 39.

134 Badiou, *Key Concepts,* 4.

135 Alain Badiou, *St. Paul: The Foundation of Universalism,* trans. Ray Brassier (Stanford: Stanford UP, 2003), 92.

136 Bartlett and Clemens, *Alain Badiou: Key Concepts,* 6.

137 Ibid., 100.

138 Ibid.

139 Bartlett and Clemens, *Alain Badiou: Key Concepts,* 100.

140 Ibid., 95.

141 Badiou, *Ethics,* xv.

142 Ibid., xii.

143 Ibid., xxxiv.

144 Ibid., 2.

145 Peter Sloterdijk, *Rage and Time,* trans. Mario Wenning (New York: Columbia UP, 2010), 184-85.

146 Bartlett and Clemens, *Alain Badiou: Key Concepts,* 146.

147 Ibid., 148.

148 Ibid., 160.

149 Ibid., 182.

150 Badiou, *Rebirth of History,* 87.

151 Ibid., 90.

152 Alain Badiou, *Philosophy for Militants,* trans. Bruno Bosteels (London: Verso, 2012), 61.

153 Badiou, *Metapolitics,* 24.

154 Alain Badiou, *Conditions*, trans. Steve Corcoran, (London: Continuum, 2008), 189.

155 Ibid., 309.

156 Badiou and Žižek, *Philosophy in the Present*, 90.

157 Badiou, *The Adventure of French Philosophy*, 95.

158 Badiou, *Ethics*, xvi.

159 Ibid., 9.

160 Susan Sontag, *Regarding the Pain of Others* (New York: Picador, 2003), 134.

161 Badiou, *Ethics*, 1.

162 Thanks to Samir Gandesha for making this link for me.

163 Badiou, *Ethics*, xi.

164 Badiou, *Polemics*, 35.

165 Badiou, *Philosophy and the Event* (London: Verso, 2013), 35.

166 Ibid., 120.

167 Ibid., 128.

168 Badiou, *Subject of Change*, 10.

169 Ibid., 50.

170 Ibid., 91.

171 Badiou, *Ethics*, 2.

172 Badiou, *Metapolitics*, 79-80.

173 Peter Hallward, *A Subject to Truth* (Minneapolis: U of Minnesota P, 2003), xxviii.

174 Alain Badiou, *Being and Event*, Oliver Feltham, tr. (London: Continuum Books, 2005), 44.

175 Hallward, *A Subject to Truth*, 100.

176 Ibid., 109.

177 Ibid., 109.

178 Ibid., 196.

179 Ibid., 314.

180 Ibid, 322.

181 Barker, *Badiou: A Critical Introduction*, 131.

182 Ibid, 70-71.

183 Taken from notes from a master class with Alain Badiou in Amsterdam, March 2012, at the Amsterdam School of Cultural Analysis.

184 Ibid.

185 Badiou, *Ethics,* 138.

186 Badiou, *Being and Event,* xvii.

187 Ibid., xxviii.

188 Ibid., xxix.

189 Ibid., xxxi.

190 Ibid., 27.

191 Ibid., 106.

192 Ibid., 111.

193 Ibid, 145.

194 Slavoj Žižek, "Against Human Rights," *libcom.org* (9 Oct. 2006) <http://libcom.org/library/against-human-rights-zizek>.

195 Ibid.

196 Ibid.

197 Badiou, *Ethics,* 13.

198 Badiou, *Communist Hypothesis,* 38.

199 Badiou, *Ethics,* 38.

200 Rebecca Solnitt: "Call climate change what it is: violence," *The Guardian* (7 April 2014) <http://www.theguardian.com/commentisfree/2014/apr/07/climate-change-violence-occupy-earth>.

201 Michael Taussig, *Shamanism, Colonialism, and the Wild Man: A Study in Terror and Healing* (Chicago: U of Chicago P, 1987), 121.

202 Taken from notes from a master class with Alain Badiou in Amsterdam, March 2012, at the Amsterdam School of Cultural Analysis.

203 Ibid.

204 Badiou, *Logics of Worlds,* 514.

205 Michel Foucault, *Society Must Be Defended: Lectures at the College de France 1975-76,* trans. David Macey (New York: Picador, 1997), 266.

206 Michel Foucault, *History of Sexuality,* 94-95.

207 Howard Caygill, *On Resistance: A Philosophy of Defiance* (London: Bloomsbury, 2013), 8.

208 Ibid., 137.

209 Badiou, *Ethics: An Essay on the Understanding of Evil,* 115-16.

210 In 'Nietzsche, Genealogy, History,' Foucault writes, "Humanity does not gradually progress from combat to combat until it arrives at universal reciprocity, where the rule of law finally replaces warfare. Humanity installs each of its violences in a system

of rules and thus proceeds from domination to domination," (Coulthard, *Red Skin, White Masks,* 25).

211 Serres, *Natural Contract,* 12.

212 Serres, *Natural Contract,* 13-14.

213 Caygill, *On Resistance: A Philosophy of Defiance,* 19.

214 Ibid., 19.

215 Ibid., 25.

216 Ibid., 28.

217 Ibid., 26.

218 Ibid., 12.

219 Gandhi's legacy is increasingly controversial due to his unwillingness to address the concerns of someone like Ambedkar in respect to the structural violence of the caste system, making his non-violence rather ambivalent (or even violent) and contributing to sealing his role in elaborating what Perry Anderson calls "Indian ideology." – Do you need a src. For this?

220 Caygill, *On Resistance: A Philosophy of Defiance,* 31.

221 Ibid., 36.

222 Caygill, *On Violence: A Philosophy of Defiance,* 91.

223 Ibid., 142-43.

224 Ibid., 144-45.

225 Ibid., 125.

226 Guy Debord, "The Sick Planet" (1971, 2004), trans. NOT BORED! (2006) (http://www.notbored.org/the-sick-planet.html).

227 Ibid.

228 Ibid.

229 Ibid.

230 Ibid.

231 Ibid.

232 Caygill, *On Resistance: A Philosophy of Defiance,* 179.

233 Giorgio Agamben, *What Is an Apparatus? and other essays* (Stanford: Stanford UP, 2009), 14.

234 Ibid., 15.

235 Ibid.

236 Ibid.,19.

237 Giorgia Agamben, *Means Without End: Notes on Politics,* trans. Vincenzo Binetti and Cesare Casarino, (Minneapolis: U of Minnesota P, 2000), 138.

238 Ibid., 24.

239 Ibid., 23.

240 Giorgio Agamben, *State of Exception*, trans. Kevin Attell (Chicago: U of Chicago P, 2005), 1.

241 Giorgio Agamben, *Homo Sacer: Sovereign Power and Bare Life*, trans. Daniel Heller-Roazen, (Stanford: Stanford UP, 1998), 19.

242 Christian Parenti, *Tropic of Chaos: Climate Change and the New Geography of Violence* (New York: Nation Books, 2011), 209.

243 Parenti, *Tropic of Chaos*, 241.

244 Ibid., 241.

245 Badiou, *Ethics: An Essay on the Understanding of Evil*, 98.

246 Glen Coulthard, "Subjects of Empire: Indigenous People and the 'Politics of Recognition' in Canada," *Contemporary Political Theory* 6 (2007): 439.

247 Hegel, qtd. in Coulthard, "Subjects of Empire," 440.

248 Coulthard, "Subjects of Empire," 440.

249 Ibid., 443.

250 Ibid., 445.

251 Ibid.

252 Frantz Fanon, *Black Skin, White Masks*, trans. Charles Lam Markmann (New York: Grove Press, 1967), 220.

253 Ibid.

254 Ibid.

255 Coulthard, "Subjects of Empire," 450-51.

256 Ibid., 451.

257 Frantz Fanon, *Wretched of the Earth*, trans. Constance Farrington (New York: Grove Press, 1963), 43.

258 Coulthard, "Subjects of Empire," 456.

259 Fanon, *Black Skin, White Masks*, 220-21.

260 Ibid., 218.

261 Ibid., 17.

262 Ibid., 23.

263 Ibid., 216

264 Ibid., 217

265 Ibid., 218.

266 Badiou, *Conditions*, 148.

267 Ibid., 150.

268 Ibid., 151.

269 Carl Schmitt, *The Nomos of the Earth,* trans. G.L. Ulmen (New York: Telos, 2003), 9.

270 Ibid., 10.

271 Ibid.

272 Ibid., 70.

273 Ibid., 15.

274 Ibid., 25.

275 Ibid.

276 Leanne Simpson, *Dancing on our Turtles Back,* (Winnipeg: Arbiter Ring Publishing, 2011), 17.

277 Ibid, 37.

278 Ibid., 42.

279 Ibid.

280 Ibid, 49.

281 Ibid., 60.

282 Ibid., 61.

283 Ibid., 66.

284 Ibid., 78-9.

285 Ibid., 87.

286 Ibid., 88.

287 Ibid., 90.

288 Ibid., 109.

289 Ibid., 108.

290 Ibid., 138.

291 Ibid, 198.

292 Ibid., 199.

293 Ibid.

294 Ibid., 226.

295 Ibid., 336.

296 Ibid.

297 Ibid., 337

298 Ibid, 352.

299 Glen Coulthard, *Red Skin, White Masks: Rejecting the Colonial Politics of Recognition,* (Minneapolis: University of Minnesota Press, 2014), 152.

300 Carl Schmitt, *The Concept of the Political,* trans. George Schwab (Chicago: University of Chicago Press, 1996), 27.

301 Ibid., 53.

302 Ibid., 19.

303 Carl Schmitt, *Political Theology,* trans. George Schwab (Chicago: University of Chicago Press, 1985), 65.

304 Ibid., 35.

305 Ibid., xxiii.

306 Schmitt, *The Concept of the Political,* 35.

307 Schmitt, *Political Theology,* 118

308 Ibid., 15.

309 Carl Schmitt, *Theory of the Partisan,* trans. G.L. Ulmen (New York: Telos, 2007), xxi.

310 Ibid., 3.

311 Ibid., 4.

312 Ibid., xii

313 Ibid., xx.

314 Ibid., 29.

315 Ibid., 22.

316 Ibid., 32.

317 Ibid., 35.

318 Ibid., 43.

319 Ibid., 48.

320 Ibid., 50.

321 Ibid., 58.

322 Ibid., 80.

323 Ibid.

324 Ibid, 90.

325 Ibid, 95.

326 Ibid, 84.

327 Ibid, 95.

328 Ibid, 95.

329 Naomi Klein, *This Changes Everything,* (Toronto: Knopf Canada, 2014), 291.

330 Carl Schmitt, *The Nomos of the Earth*, 86.

331 Michel Foucault, *Security, Territory, Population 1977-78*, trans. Graham Burchell (New York: Picador, 2007), 5.

332 Ibid., 1.

333 Henri Lefebvre, *The Production of Space*, trans. Donald Nicholson-Smith (Oxford: Blackwell, 1974), 116.

334 Giorgio Agamben, *Means Without End: Notes on Politics.*

335 Žižek, *Living in the End Times*, 360.

336 Benjamin Bratton qtd. in Carla Leitao, "Designing Geopolitics," *Huffington Post* (10 July 2012) <http://www.huffingtonpost.com/carla-leitao/designing-geopolitics_b_1658037.html>.

337 Refers to phenomenon that are massively distributed in time and space relative to humans in Timothy Morton, *Hyperobjects*, (Minneapolis: University of Minnesota Press, 2013), 1.

338 Zbigniew Brzezinski, *Between Two Ages: America's Role in the Technetronic Era* (New York: Viking Press, 1970), 97.

339 Zbigniew Brzezinski, *The Grand Chessboard* (New York: Basic Books, 1997), 40.

340 Zbigniew Brzezinski, *The Choice: Global Domination or Global Leadership* (New York: Basic Books, 2004), 2006-07.

341 Eyal Weizman, *Hollow Land: Israel's Architecture of Occupation* (London: Verso, 2007), 188.

342 Fredric Jameson, "Notes on the Nomos," *South Atlantic Quarterly* 104.2 (Spring 2005), 204.

343 Benjamin Bratton, "On the Nomos of the Cloud," talk presented at the Berlage Institute, Rotterdam, 28 November 2011 <https://www.youtube.com/watch?v=XDRxNO-JxXEE>.

344 Ibid.

345 Benjamin Bratton, "Some Trace Effects of the Post-Anthropocene: On Accelerationist Geopolitical Aesthetics," *e-flux Journal* 46. Is this the page number of the printed issue, if not, include the URL and date of publication.

346 Bratton, "On the Nomos of the Cloud." (http://bratton.info/projects/talks/on-the-nomos-of-the-cloud-the-stack-deep-address-integral-geography/)

347 Ibid.

348 Ibid.

349 Bratton, "Some Trace Effects of the Post-Anthropocene: On Accelerationist Geopolitical Aesthetics." 2013 e-flux: http://www.e-flux.com/journal/some-trace-effects-of-the-post-anthropocene-on-accelerationist-geopolitical-aesthetics/

350 Ibid.

351 Ibid.

352 Ibid.

353   Geoff Mann and Joel Wainwright, *Climate Leviathan, Antipode* Vol. 00 No. 0 2012 ISSN 0066-4812, pp 1–22 .

354 Walter Benjamin, *On the Concept of History,* trans. Dennis Redmond, Gesammelten Schriften I:2, Suhrkamp Verlag. Frankfurt am Main, 1974).

355 Bratton, "On the Nomos of the Cloud." (http://bratton.info/projects/talks/on-the-nomos-of-the-cloud-the-stack-deep-address-integral-geography/)

356 Bratton, "Some Trace Effects of the Post-Anthropocene." e-flux 2013: http://www.e-flux.com/journal/some-trace-effects-of-the-post-anthropocene-on-accelerationist-geopolitical-aesthetics/

357 Bratton, "On the Nomos of the Cloud." (http://bratton.info/projects/talks/on-the-nomos-of-the-cloud-the-stack-deep-address-integral-geography/)

358 Bratton, "Some Trace Effects of the Post-Anthropocene." e-flux: http://www.e-flux.com/journal/some-trace-effects-of-the-post-anthropocene-on-accelerationist-geopolitical-aesthetics/

359 Ibid.

360 Ibid.

361 Ibid.

362 Talk by Benjamin Bratton at Simon Fraser University, Oct. 29th, 2014 – available: http://www.sfu.ca/video-library/video/854/view.html

363 Quentin Meillassoux, *After Finitude: An Essay on the Necessity of Contingency,* trans. Ray Brassier (London: Continuum, 2008), 48.

364 Ibid., 20.

365 Žižek, *Living in the End Times,* 327.

366 For Serres, "The prophet overthrew the king. Science takes the place of law and establishes its tribunals, whose judgments, henceforth, will make those of other authorities seem arbitrary. And now, what are we to do and how are we to decide, by what right, in a world and a time that only knows how to know and only does that which ensues knowledge? A world which science alone is believed." (Serres, *The Natural Contract,* 86).

367 Karl Marx, "On the Question of Free Trade," *Karl Marx: Selected Writings,* trans. David MacLellan, (Oxford: Oxford University Press, 2000), 296.

368 Gilles Deleuze and Felix Guattari, *Accelerate: Accelerationist Reader,* eds. Robin Mackay and Armen Avanessian (Falmouth: Urbanomic, 2014), 162.

369 Alex Williams, "Escape Velocities," *e-flux journal* 46 (June 2013).

370 Ibid.

371 Robin Mackay and Armen Avanessian, "Power of Repetition," *#Accelerate#:*

The Accelerationist Reader, eds. Robin Mackay and Armen Avanessian (Falmouth: Urbanomic, 2014), 30.

372 Franco "Bifo" Berardi, "Accelerationism Questioned from the Point of View of the Body," *e-flux journal* 46 (June 2013).

373 Benedict Singleton, "Maximum Jailbreak," *#Accelerate#: The Accelerationist Reader*, ed. Robin Mackay and Armen Avanessian (Falmouth: Urbanomic, 2014), 494-95.

374 Gene Moreno, *Editorial, e-*flux journal #46, June 2013. URL

375 Gilles Lipovetsky, "Power of Repetition," *#Accelerate#: The Accelerationist Reader*, eds. Robin Mackay and Armen Avenessian (Falmouth: Urbanomic Media Ltd., 2014), 226-27.

376 Patricia Reed, "Seven Prescriptions for Accelerationism," *#Accelerate#: The Accelerationist Reader*, eds. Robin Mackay and Armen Avanessian, (Falmouth, Urbanomic, 2014), 526-27.

377 Ibid, 530.

378 Clive Hamilton, *Climate Change Geoengineering: Philosophical Perspectives, Legal Issues, and Governance Frameworks*, ed. Wil C. G. Burns and Andrew L. Strauss (Cambridge: Cambridge University Press, 2013), 39.

379 David Harvey, *Justice, Nature and the Geography of Difference* (Oxford: Blackwell, 1996), 184.

380 Neil Smith, *Uneven Development: Nature, Capital, and the Production of Space* (Athens: University of Georgia Press, 1984), 32.

381 Ibid, 35.

382 Ibid, 37.

383 Ibid, 90.

384 Ibid, 123.

385 Smith, *Uneven Development*, 11.

386 Adorno, T. W., with Max Horkheimer. *Dialectic of Enlightenment*. Trans. Edmund Jephcott. Stanford: Stanford University Press, 2002. 113.

387 Karl Marx, *Grundrisse*, trans. Martin Nicolaus (London: Penguin, 1993), 489.

388 Frederick Engels, "Outlines of a Critique of Political Economy," in *Karl Marx, The Economic and Philosophic Manuscripts of 1844*, as cited in Howard Parsons, ed., *Marx and Engels on Ecology* (Westport, CT: Greenwood Press, 1977), 210.

389 John Bellamy Foster, *Marx's Ecology: Materialism and Nature* (New York: Monthly Review Press, 2000), 157.

390 Ibid., 155-56.

391 Ibid., 157.

392 Ibid., 158.

393 Ibid., 226.

394 Ibid., 240-41.

395 John Bellamy Foster, Brett Clark and Richard York, *The Ecological Rift: Capitalism's War on Earth,* (New York: Monthly Review Press, 2010), 28.

396 Ibid., 60.

397 Ibid., 123.

398 Ibid., 284.

399 Friedrich Nietzsche, *Portable Nietzsche,* trans. Walter Kaufman (New York: Viking Penguin, 1954), 42.

400 Andrew Biro, ed. *Critical Ecologies: The Frankfurt School and Contemporary Environmental Crises,* (Toronto: University of Toronto Press, 2011), 229.

401 Žižek, *Living in the End Times,* 330.

402 Karl Marx, *Fragment on Machines, #Accelerate#: The Accelerationist Reader,* eds. Robin MacKay and Armen Avanessian (Falmouth: Urbanomic, 2014), 53.

403 David Harvey, *Seventeen Contradictions and the End of Capitalism* (Oxford: Oxford University Press, 2014), 208.

404 Ibid., 219.

405 Ibid., 246.

406 Ibid., 259.

407 Ibid., 262.

408 Ibid., 265.

409 Thank you to Samir Gandesha for offering this observation during an early reading.

410 Neil Smith, *Uneven Development: Nature, Capital and the Production of Space,* (Athens, University of Georgia, 1984), 8.

411 Sigmund Freud, *The Standard Edition of the Complete Psychological Works of Sigmund Freud, Vol. XIV,* ed. J. Strachey (London: Hogarth Press, 1956), 307.

412 Walter Benjamin, *Illuminations: Essays and Reflections,* 123.

413 Peter Sloterdijk, *Bubbles: Spheres I,* trans. Wieland Hoban (Cambridge: MIT Press, 2011), 27.

414 Ibid., 46.

415 Peter Sloterdijk and Hans-Jürgen Heinrichs, *Neither Sun Nor Death,* trans. Steve Corcoran, (Los Angeles: Semiotext(e), 2001), 14.

416 Schirmacher, Wolfgang. "Technoculture and Life Technique." In: Wolfgang Schirmacher. *Just Living. Philosophy in Artificial Life.* Atropos Press. New York, Dresden. ISBN 0981946269.

417 Ibid.

418 Ibid.

419 Ibid.

420 Martin Heidegger, *Being and Time,* trans. John Macquarrie and Edward Robinson (New York: Harper and Row), 44.

421 Richard Wolin, *The Heidegger Controversy: Only a God Can Save Us* (Cambridge, MIT Press, 1992), 107.

422 Serres, *The Natural Contract,* 25.

423 Ibid., 12.

424 Ibid,. 11.

425 Serres, *The Natural Contract,* 25.

426 Biro, *Critical Ecologies: The Frankfurt School and Contemporary Environmental Crises,* 15.

427 Ibid., 59.

428 Ibid., 80.

429 Ibid., 82.

430 Ibid., 118.

431 Ibid., 123.

432 Ibid., 125.

433 Ibid., 125.

434 Ibid., 141.

435 Schmitt, *Theory of the Partisan,* 80.

436 Based on notes from Alain Badiou masterclass at Amsterdam School of Cultural Analysis, University of Amsterdam, March 2013.

437 Fanon, *The Wretched of the Earth,* 36.

438 Guy Debord, "The Sick Planet."

439 Peter Sloterdijk, *Terror from the Air,* trans. Amy Patton and Steve Corcoran (Los Angeles: Semiotext(e), 2009), 50.

440 Ibid., 65.

441 Joseph Conrad, *Heart of Darkness* (London: Dover Thrift Editions, 1990), 65.

442 From a talk by Dr. Gwynne Dyer at Simon Fraser University in Vancouver, Canada, Nov. 2013.

443 Parenti, *Climate Change and the New Geography of Violence,* 15.

444 Ibid., 27.

445 Michael Specter, "The Climate Fixers," *The New Yorker* (4 May 2012). <http://www.newyorker.com/reporting/2012/05/14/120514fa_fact_specter?currentPage=all>.

446 Ibid.

447 Ibid.

448 Ibid.

449 Ibid.

450 Definition presented by the Royal Society in the UK: <https://royalsociety.org/policy/publications/2009/geoengineering-climate/>.

451 Stephen Gardiner, *Climate Change Geoengineering: Philosophical Perspectives, Legal Issues and Governance Frameworks,* ed. Wil C. G. Burn and Andrew L. Strauss (Cambridge: Cambridge UK, 2013), 2.

452 Zoe McKnight, "B.C. company at centre of iron dumping scandal stands by its convictions," *The Vancouver Sun* (4 Sept. 2013) <http://www.vancouversun.com/technology/company+centre+iron+dumping+scandal+stands+convictions/8860731/story.html>.

453 Clive Hamilton, *Climate Change Geoengineering: Philosophical Perspectives, Legal Issues, and Governance Frameworks,* ed. Wil C. G. Burns and Andrew L. Strauss (Cambridge: Cambridge University Press, 2013), 51.

454 Ibid., 57.

455 Ibid., 53, fn. 50.

456 Naomi Klein, *This Changes Everything,* (Toronto: Alfred A Knopf Canada, 2014), 279.

457 Michael Specter, "The Climate Fixers," *The New Yorker* (4 May 2012) <http://www.newyorker.com/reporting/2012/05/14/120514fa_fact_specter?currentPage=all>.

458 Hamilton, *Climate Change Geoengineering,* 57.

459 Jay Michaelson, *Climate Change Geoengineering: Philosophical Perspectives, Legal Issues, and Governance Frameworks,* ed. Wil C. G. Burns and Andrew L. Strauss (Cambridge: Cambridge University Press, 2013), 96.

460 Sloterdijk, *Terror from the Air,* 86.

461 Lipscomb in Biro, "Critical Ecologies," 278.

462 Benjamin Bratton, "Some Trace Effects of the Anthropocene: On Accelerationist Geopolitical Aesthetics," *e-flux journal* 46 (June 2013) <http://www.e-flux.com/journal/some-trace-effects-of-the-post-anthropocene-on-accelerationist-geopolitical-aesthetics/>.

463 Lipscomb in Biro, "Critical Ecologies," 286.

464 Patricia Reed, *#Accelerate#: The Accelerationist Reader*, eds. Robin Mackay and Armen Avanessian (Falmouth: Urbanomic, 2014), 532.

465 Badiou, *Logics of Worlds,* 508.

466 Derrida's antidote to this was to suggest that "Monsters cannot be announced. One cannot say: 'here are our monsters', without immediately turning the monsters into

pets." See "Some Statements and Truisms about Neologisms, Newisms, Postisms, Para-sitisms, and other small Seismisms," *The States of Theory*, ed. David Carroll (New York: Columbia University Press, 1989).

467 Badiou, *Theory of the Subject*, 509.

468 Serres, *The Natural Contract*, 58.

Think Media: EGS Media Philosophy Series

Wolfgang Schirmacher, *editor*

Other books available from Atropos Press

5 Milton Stories (For the Witty, Wise and Worldly Child), Sofia Fasos Korahais

Che Guevara and the Economic Debate in Cuba, Luiz Bernardo Pericás

Grey Ecology, Paul Virilio

heart, speech, this, Gina Rae Foster

Follow Us or Die, Vincent W.J., van Gerven Oei

Just Living: Philosophy in Artificial Life. Collected Works Volume 1, Wolfgang Schirmacher

Laughter, Henri Bergson

Pessoa, The Meaphysical Courier, Judith Balso

Philosophical Essays: from Ancient Creed to Technological Man, Hans Jonas

Philosophy of Culture, Schopenhauer and Tradition, Wolfgang Schirmacher

Talking Cheddo: Teaching Hard Kushitic Truths Liberating PanAfrikanism, Menkowra Manga Clem Marshall

Teletheory, Gregory L. Ulmer

The Tupperware Blitzkrieg, Anthony Metivier

Vilém Flusser's Brazilian Vampyroteuthis Infernalis, Vilém Flusser

New Releases from Atropos Press

Beyond Reflection, Anders Kolle

HARDSCAPE/ABC, Andrew Spano

Hermeneutics of New Modernism, Lisa Paul Streitfeld

The Image Is Crisis, Nancy Jones

Languages of Resistance, Maya Nitis

Nanotexts, Tony Prichard

Media, Meaning, & the Legitimation Problem from the Eradication of the Meta Narrative to the Present, Gregory O'Toole

Media Psychology, Matthew Tyler Giobbi

On Techne of Authority: Political Economy in a Digital Age, G. M. Bell

On Leaving: Poetry, Daesthetics, Timelessness, Lori Martindale

On Fidelity; Or, Will You Still Love Me Tomorrow..., Jeremy Fernando

Surfgeist: Narratives of Epic Mythology in New Media, Peggy Ann Bloomer

www.ingramcontent.com/pod-product-compliance
Lightning Source LLC
LaVergne TN
LVHW022318060326
832902LV00020B/3530

*9 7 8 1 9 4 0 8 1 3 9 2 9 *